Finding
Home
within the
HEART of
the EARTH

About the Author

Eagle Skyfire is a respected elder and spiritual teacher with over thirty years' experience in helping people find their life purpose and meaningful growth in their personal spiritual journeys while sharing the traditions she has learned from various Native American spiritual teachers. Her hands-on, practical approach is successful in assisting countless people in a wide range of ways, such as developing their intuitive and shamanic skills, creating personal spiritual practices, understanding past lives, and soul work. Many people from around the world seek her for readings on personal and professional matters, connecting with loved ones who have crossed over, communicating with animals, and interpreting dreams and visions.

Over the years she has been asked to share her knowledge at various community and professional events as a cultural and spiritual presenter. Eagle Skyfire has guided many people to manifest healthier and whole lives.

On her website, www.eagleskyfire.com, she has a popular blog called *Flow of the River*, where she shares what she interprets from the sacred flow of energy around us. Many people look forward to this guidance on a weekly basis. She also directs a live local radio talk show on WCHE 1520 AM called *Fresh Perspective*, in which she provides an overview of the *Flow of the River* and welcomes callers every Monday.

EAGLE SKYFIRE

Finding Home
within the
HEART of
the EARTH

CREATING
a
HARMONIOUS
SPACE

with the
ENERGY

of the
EARTH

Llewellyn Publications
Woodbury, Minnesota

FIRST EDITION
First Printing, 2020

Cover design by Shira Atakpu
Interior art by the Llewellyn Art Department

Llewellyn Publications is a registered trademark of Llewellyn Worldwide Ltd.

Library of Congress Cataloging-in-Publication Data (Pending)
ISBN: 978-0-7387-6066-7

Llewellyn Publications
A Division of Llewellyn Worldwide Ltd.
2143 Wooddale Drive
Woodbury, MN 55125-2989
www.llewellyn.com

Printed in the United States of America

OTHER BOOKS BY EAGLE SKYFIRE

Journeying Between the Worlds: Walking with the Sacred Spirits Through Native American Shamanic Teachings & Practices

I dedicate this book to all of you who seek to grow greater peace and joy within your hearts and within your homes while seeking to live in greater harmony with the natural world. By striving to do this you help to make the world a better place and help to heal our environment for future generations.

CONTENTS

EXERCISES

Acknowledgments

Thank you Great Spirit for the gift of my life and all of the experiences that I have been granted in order to grow in wisdom and deeper understanding. Thank you to Earth Mother and to All My Relations, for it is in your beauty, the beauty of the natural world, that inspires me and, in turn, allows for all of us to remember that we are one planet, one people, one creation. I give thanks to my helpers seen and unseen, for as I go about my daily business, I realize that every step of every day is sacred. I also extend my gratitude to my teachers on the Good Red Road as well as my clients, students, family, and friends that give me feedback and insights that I otherwise would have missed. I would also like to thank all at Llewellyn Worldwide, especially my editors, who with their tireless help and patient guidance brought this book into being. I am very grateful to you, dear reader, for as you read this book and bring the Heart of the Earth Mother into your living spaces, you help to bring more beauty to life and make our world a better and happier place.

DISCLAIMER

It is my honor to share these teachings with you, and they are meant to empower you. However, completing them does not make you a shaman, adopt you officially into any tribe, nor give you the authorization to perform the Heart of the Earth method for others. This book barely scratches the surface of what is required to be able to give shamanic or professional advice to others in relation to clearing or setting up another person's environment, living space, or work place. Becoming a sanctioned traditional shaman takes many years of constant training under the careful guidance of a shaman and tribal elders. You would need to be trained in this technique before you could advise others. Trying to perform any of the exercises or techniques that I am giving you here for other people may cause great harm to you and to them! Please do not attempt these techniques for anyone else besides yourself or those who share your home, work space, or dorm. Eagle Skyfire; Eagle Skyfire, LLC; and Llewellyn Worldwide are not liable for any damages sustained—mental, physical, or spiritual—in conjunction to using this book. Safety always comes first. Use your common sense when applying the Heart of the Earth method.

INTRODUCTION

BEING IN A SPACE WHERE we feel at home allows us to relax and be fully present. In a work place, this can be of tremendous benefit because it can allow for a group of people to feel that they have an environment conducive to supporting them in their joint endeavors. It turns a house into a home, and because the space becomes a sanctuary, it will allow you to restore your vitality, safely release the tensions of the day, and nurture yourself while envisioning how you want to build your future.

This book and the Heart of the Earth method—a way of living in harmony with the earth—was born out of my careful observation of people's needs and that of their families and animal companions. I see a great need around me as I see people desire to create a safe place that they can call their own. For quite a few decades now I have been to countless places and successfully helped people clear these spaces of unwanted, toxic energies, resetting them so that they can promote greater health, harmony, and productivity. All too many times I have seen people feel completely disconnected from their environment, which in turn causes them to be nervous and stressed, and causes tension among each other.

I have had many requests from people who wanted me to teach them how to do this method for themselves. This is why I have written this book to be a simple hands-on, step-by-step guide in order to enhance harmony, wellness, and overall greater sense of well-being in many environments.

People have asked me if this is like feng shui, the Chinese practice of arranging spaces for harmony. It is not. Over the years I have developed my own system that is a synthesis of Native American spiritual principles and shamanic practices, current resources, wisdom gained from experiences in the field, and my intuitive gifts. This book will instruct you on basic exercises and techniques to guide you into making any space your own so that you may get the maximum benefit from it.

TRADITION ORIGIN

While I was born into a multigenerational South American indigenous tradition, it is not something that I was formally taught as part of my regular upbringing because it was thought to be unnecessary in this modern age. Over the years my natural inclination toward the sacred practices became very evident. It ultimately led me to be adopted by a powerful spirit man, Ted Silverhand, who is of the Tuscarora Nation and Bear clan, and into the traditions he follows.

Over the years it has been my privilege to learn from Native American teachers from many nations. When I was very young, about eight to ten years old, I was taught the ways of the Tuscarora people. As I grew older, I was granted permission to receive teachings from the Seneca, Anishinaabe, the Cherokee, and a little from the Lakota Nations. As I continued my walk through the

Americas I received wisdom from the Taino, Inca, and Maya. I was granted permission from all my Medicine Teachers to share what was given to me. I write to the universal Heart of the Good Red Road to respect individual tribes, for only they can determine with whom to share their unique ceremonies. My experiences afford me a distinctive view not only of the commonalities of Native American spiritualities and uniqueness that each tribe holds, but how these ancient teachings are still relevant today.

This book, and the Heart of the Earth method, is the synthesis of combining my life's wisdom, time-honored techniques, and Native American spiritual principles. Its purpose is to give you tools that you may apply to your everyday environment and living space.

BENEFITS

Using Heart of the Earth techniques creates an energy that everyone will respond to whether they are conscious of it or not. You will benefit from greater harmony with your environment and within yourself.

This method has brought much abundance, peace, and contentment to the places that I have applied it to throughout the years. It is my hope that as you connect and harmonize with nature, your Sacred Self, and the spirit of the space, work space, or home, these techniques will bring you contentment. Using the method of the Heart of the Earth you will create a naturally harmonious, unique, and very personal haven for you and for those whom you love.

Another benefit that you will receive from living in greater harmony with the Heart of the Earth is that of attracting benevolent spirits to your place. Don't be surprised if you see earth spirits, which in Western cultures are known as fae or fairies. These spirit beings can be very protective of the ones whom they reside with. They can be very helpful but need to be given ground rules. Typically, you will find objects appearing and disappearing at random, but never in a harmful way.

Other spirits that might come are the Sacred Ancestors of the Land. These are divine spirits that are part of the land itself. Some of them are indigenous spirits who come because they can sense that you wish to work in harmony and with greater respect to the earth and with all beings. The Sacred Ancestors of the Land are benevolent protectors and they bless and enhance the overall feeling of serenity and contentment wherever they are. It is not uncommon for them to share their wisdom by giving you good advice and to comfort you in times of need. The Sacred Ancestors of the Land only come to those who truly have goodwill and compassion as their way of being.

It is not only good spiritual Beings that will be attracted to you. You will find that your wild neighbors will be enticed to visit you too! Now before you get excited, what I mean by this is the birds and the animals will be drawn to your place even if you do not offer food or water. They come because they can feel that your place is safe and tranquil. Of course, if you wish to offer food and drink to them, this is a good way of honoring them. It is a great way to thank them for the songs that they sing or sounds that they make that make you smile, plus the gifts of inspiration and joy as you see them when you are sitting outside.

When and How to Use This Book

These techniques are meant to be used by anyone who wants to improve their space by making the energy more harmonious with nature, and with the people and animals who also share that space with them. The Heart of the Earth method can be applied whether you are looking for a new place or updating an existing one.

As we all know, life is a series of cycles and changes. Transitions that affect our lifestyles can happen to us at any time. At times they are planned, like that of a graduation, wedding, the birth of a child, or a change of career. And other times it can happen suddenly through the death of a loved one, a redefining or downsizing of a job, or the growing demands of caregiving for a relative. Major stressful transitions such as that of death, sudden loss, or divorce can force us into releasing our old lives whether we are ready for it or not and put us in a position of needing to reinvent ourselves for the future.

Using the Heart of the Earth method can give you the tools you need in order to be able to "go with the flow" with changes that life brings, whether the changes are planned or not. A space that will be nourishing and supportive mentally, physically, emotionally, and spiritually for all will be created when factoring in your resources, your needs, and the likes and dislikes of those who will also be affected by the space.

Please note, however, that this book only scratches the surface of this technique. I am giving you a solid foundation so that you can use all that you read within these pages with confidence and safety in order to improve your overall quality of life. Developing this method to help others took me several decades of using my shamanic skills and being able to interpret the nuances of nature, human needs, and how they interact with each other while out in the field.

Trying to do these techniques for others without proper training may result in accidentally creating disruptive or even harmful effects! For areas that require more knowledge than you may have it is wise to contact someone of skill or who is a professional in their field, such as an interior decorator, handyman, electrician, or, if necessary, someone who does more intense spiritual cleansing.

This book works best if you read it through completely from beginning to end, but I have written it so that you can jump to different sections individually depending on your circumstances. We are living beings who are ever growing and changing and since our environments are an extension of ourselves, the energy and items within them should reflect this too. It is my hope that you will enjoy this book and that the Heart of the Earth method will help you gain greater confidence in using your creativity to develop your personal spaces. It will teach you how to make better choices of what to bring into your environment by respectfully connecting with our beloved Earth Mother and all of the people and animals that share your life.

I have written this book so you may go as lightly or as in-depth as you desire to. If it is a case where you would only like to do a blessing or a light spiritual cleansing, then you can do that. If you would like to merely tweak what you have in order to improve what is already there, you can do that too. Or, if you wish to go "all in" and start from the ground up to completely craft your space or rebuild it from scratch, this book will give you the tools so you can complete that task. This book is user-friendly so you can approach it for whatever your needs are at the time and at the level that you want to align your space to be in harmony with nature and with the stage of life you are in.

For ease of reference this book is broken into two parts. The first part introduces basic concepts and the second part is focused on the actual creation of your space. Throughout both parts I have many exercises that will heighten your senses and sharpen your skills so you can be confident with interpreting your findings and how to apply them properly. Figures and charts are provided throughout for quick reference in relation to the Medicine Wheel, the compass points, and more.

Part one will cover basic definitions and vocabulary that are required for you to be able to use this technique effectively. I talk about why we need to reconnect with the natural world in addition to explaining universal Native American spiritual concepts. There are also fundamental energetic principles that you need to understand so that you can apply the techniques that will come in part two. I will point out the importance of having the proper mental attitude and finding your center because these play a pivotal role in successfully creating your space. I also go into detail of the different features of the land—both physical and energetic—and how this impacts you.

Part two focuses on evaluating, planning, and creating your space. I will guide you on how to clearly define what you want from your home or work space regardless if it is a new place or one that you are updating to meet your current needs. I will give you a quick way to evaluate if a place is correct for you if you are hunting for a new one. I will also cover, in detail, the qualities of each of the directions, assessing your property, and the function of each room in relation to the five elements. You will learn how to set the Heart of your place, which sets the energetic tone and maintains the health of your home or work place. I touch on practical advice for crafting your space, such as the use of light and color, culling clutter, and welcoming sacred Beings into your place. I share simple rituals to establish and sustain good spiritual energy in your home or work space. Finally, I will instruct you on how to maintain your place so that it remains healthy and current, in addition to sharing recommended resources.

After reading through the chapters, a good place to begin honing your skills is by rereading the initial exercises in chapter three on heightening your senses—Way of the Sage and Way of the Warrior—so that you can understand and feel the energetic features of your place. The same is true when developing another basic skill found in chapter seven, which is learning how to bless things and clear them properly with the ancient ritual of smudging. Because I know there could be restrictions or respiratory difficulties, I also give you a smokeless alternative for this ceremony. These are essential skills that will benefit you regardless of the level of involvement that you wish to have when aligning your residence or place of business with the Heart of the Earth method.

At times you may notice that certain words are capitalized that are not normally. This is to differentiate something as honorific or sacred versus mundane. For example, the Seven Arrows are a sacred collective of divine Beings versus seven arrows that are projectiles you would sling from a bow.

Please take time to orient yourself with this book and think in advance as to what you wish to accomplish. It will make it much easier to streamline the process and make it much more enjoyable.

PART 1
Basic Concepts

One

WHY WE NEED
CONTACT WITH NATURE

❧

ALL TOO OFTEN WHEN we think about what might be impacting us when we are feeling uncomfortable or unsettled there is a tendency to only look at the human interactions. There is, however, another factor that, although seemingly invisible, is all around us at all times. This is our environment. It is my belief that what we do to ourselves we also do to our environment and our Earth Mother. It also goes the other way: what we do to our environment and Earth Mother we do to ourselves.

In Native American spiritualities, it is said that all things are made by the sacred energy and Breath of the Creator. It is through this universal energy that all things can manifest. Our Ancestors, regardless of our origins, in ancient times had to take heed of the natural world. Not doing so could create countless hardships upon a clan or tribe. Being out of sync with the cycles of the seasons could be far more severe than merely being inconvenienced. It could result in the death of a village or of a whole population within a region.

It is only in relatively recent times that people have forgotten that we are still deeply reliant and still need to remain profoundly respectful of our beautiful planet and the other creatures who walk upon it with us. Because of this disconnect, we have been misusing our resources and now our planet suffers from oceans that are polluted with plastics, soil that is so depleted it produces crops that are not as nutritious as they used to be, and accelerated global climate change.

It is not only our planet that suffers from our disconnection. When we see ourselves as separate from our environment and from nature, we become unhealthy. Depression, anxiety, disease, and even strife in relationships can arise when we feel that the environment we are in is not conducive to feeling safe enough to sustain positive growth.

So important is our need to be in touch with nature in some way that in 2005 journalist Richard Louv coined the phrase nature-deficit disorder in his seventh book, *Last Child in the Woods: Saving Our Children from Nature-Deficit Disorder*.[1] Although it is not a clinical diagnosis, this book detailed the importance of being in connection with nature in some fashion, especially when it comes to healthy childhood development. The more time we spend indoors without spending time in nature makes us feel alienated to the world around us and with each other. Being out of sync with the elements of nature makes us more vulnerable to negative moods and can have major negative impacts on our overall health of spirit, body, and mind. Although it is not a medical diagnosis, it is a very good metaphor for what

---

1. Richard Louv, *Last Child in the Woods: Saving Our Children from Nature-Deficit Disorder* (Chapel Hill, North Carolina: Algonquin Books, 2005).

happens to us as individuals and as a community when we lose our connection with the greater web of life.

Everything that you see, hear, and feel impacts the various body systems, in addition to influencing your mood. Separation from nature increases blood pressure, heart rate, muscle tension, and stimulates the production of cortisol and other stress hormones. Scientists explain that we are "hardwired" to be biophiles.[2] This means that we, as a species, have an innate need to be in contact with nature in some way for our well-being. So deep-rooted is our relationship with the natural world that we actually heal faster from injuries when exposed to it.

It is because of these reasons that in the 1980s Japan adopted a practice called "shinrin-yoku."[3] It translates to "taking in the forest atmosphere" or "forest bathing." The researchers found medical evidence of unexpected benefits that go way beyond that of reducing blood pressure. In addition to providing ample amounts of oxygen the trees also produce a substance called phytoncides—natural oils that are part of a plant's defense system against

2. Judith Heerwagen, "Biophilia, Health, and Well-Being," *Restorative Commons: Creating Health and Well-Being through Urban Landscapes,* eds. Lindsay Campbell and Anne Wiesen (New Town Square, PA: USDA Forest Service, 2009), 38–57, https://www.nrs.fs.fed.us/pubs/gtr/gtr-nrs-p -39papers/04-heerwagen-p-39.pdf; Cecily. J. Maller, Claire Henderson -Wilson, and Mardie Townsend, "Rediscovering Nature in Everyday Settings: Or How to Create Healthy Environments and Healthy People," *EcoHealth* 6, no. 4 (December 2009): 553–56, https://doi.org/ 10.1007 /s10393-010-0282-5.

3. Association of Nature and Forest Therapy Guides and Programs, "What is Forest Therapy?," accessed July 7, 2020, https://www.natureandforesttherapy .org/about/the-practice-of-forest-therapy; Ephrat Livni, "The Japanese Practice of 'Forest Bathing' Is Scientifically Proven to Improve Your Health," Quartz, October 12, 2016, https://qz.com/804022 /health-benefits-japanese-forest-bathing/.

bacteria, insects, and fungi. Exposure to these substances has measurable health benefits for humans. There is a study that observes that when individuals breathe the natural organic exhalations of the trees, it strengthens their own bodies and immune systems. Breathing in these organic compounds produced by the trees supports our "NK" (natural killer) cells that are part of our immune system's way of fighting cancer.[4]

Researchers Frances E. Kuo and Andrea Faber Taylor are both children's environment and behavior researchers at the University of Illinois in Urbana-Champaign. The two conducted a study with children diagnosed with ADHD. In the study these children participated in an activity, such as walking or reading, for twenty minutes in various environments. The environments ranged from urban places to those that were "green," such as a field or forest path. They would then perform different studies to test the effects of those various environments on the children's ADHD. After analyzing the results of her experiment Kuo and Taylor concluded that children with ADHD, regardless of gender or background, received greater benefits from a natural setting by having a significant reduction in their ADHD symptoms, the most notable being a much greater increase in their attention

---

4. Karin Evans, "Why Forest Bathing Is Good for Your Health," *Greater Good Magazine,* August 20, 2018, https://greatergood.berkeley.edu/article/item /why_forest_bathing_is_good_for_your_health; Yuko Tsunetsugu, Bum-Jin Park, and Yoshifumi Miyazaki. "Trends in Research Related to 'Shinrin-yoku' (Taking In the Forest Atmosphere or Forest Bathing) in Japan," *Environmental Health and Preventive Medicine* 15, no. 27 (July 2009), https:// doi.org/10.1007/s12199-009-0091-z.

spans and a substantial decrease of hyperactivity after spending time in a green environment.[5]

These beneficial effects go beyond affecting individuals and can have positive impact on a collective of people as well. Another field study at the University of Illinois observed an interesting phenomenon in regards to residents living in Chicago public housing. The study compared residents who had easy access to or were within sight of trees and green space versus residents surrounded only by buildings and concrete.[6] Those who had access to green space in some form reported knowing more people, had stronger feelings of community with their neighbors, and had more empathy and concern with helping and supporting each other. It was also noted that in neighborhoods without trees the crime rate was higher. There were increased levels of violence and aggression between persons living in these treeless environments and the same was seen amongst domestic partners in these neighborhoods.

The researchers studied the MRI images of participants who volunteered for the test. This medical exam was used to measure brain activities of participants when they viewed nature scenes and green spaces versus when they did not. The part of the brain

5. Frances E. Kuo and Andrea Faber Taylor, "A Potential Natural Treatment for Attention-Deficit/Hyperactivity Disorder: Evidence From a National Study," *American Journal of Public Health* 94, no. 9 (September 1, 2004): 1580–1586, https://doi.org/10.2105/AJPH.94.9.1580; Martha Driessnack, "Children and Nature-Deficit Disorder," *Journal for Specialists in Pediatric Nursing* 14, no. 1 (January 2009): 73–75, https://search.proquest.com /openview /a987ec02528b8b51140c9486b2ff8431/1?pq -origsite=gscholar&cbl=25318.

6. Frances E. Kuo and William C. Sullivan, "Environment and Crime In the Inner City: Does Vegetation Reduce Crime?," *Environment and Behavior* 33, no. 3 (May 1, 2001): 343–367, https://doi.org/10.1177/0013916501333002.

that is associated with empathy and love became much more stimulated and lit up when they were looking at images of the natural world. However, when the same volunteers gazed upon urban scenes that were devoid of trees or green areas the regions of the brain associated with fear and anxiety were strongly activated.

Even in the city, being exposed to nature in some way gives people the ability to cope with life's stresses and hardships, especially when living in poverty.[7] This increased feeling of peace makes us more inclined to be receptive and empathetic to each other. It also makes us aware of being more considerate and spurs us to acts of kindness and compassion for ourselves, others, and our planet.

Fortunately, these benefits can still be felt even if one does not have the ability to go out into a natural or green environment. A study conducted by physician Robert Ulrich on patients who had successfully undergone gallbladder surgery demonstrates this.[8] Half of the patients had a view of trees and nature and the rest only had a view of blank wall. Patients with the ability to see the trees tolerated pain better and had fewer complications. They were also discharged more quickly than those who only had a wall to look at. Similar effects were noted when pictures of nature

7. Ming Kuo, William Sullivan, Rebekah Coley, and Liesette Brunson, "Fertile Ground for Community: Inner-City Neighborhood Common Spaces," *American Journal of Community Psychology* 26, no. 6 (December 1998): 823–51, https://doi.org/10.1023/A:1022294028903; Danielle F. Shanahan, Richard A. Fuller, Robert Bush, Brenda B. Lin, and Kevin J. Gaston, "The Health Benefits of Urban Nature: How Much Do We Need?," *BioScience* 65, no. 5 (April 2015): 476–85, https://doi.org/10.1093/biosci/biv032.

8. Roger S. Ulrich, "View Through a Window May Influence Recovery from Surgery," *Science* 224 (April 27, 1984): 420–22, https://pdfs.semanticscholar.org/43df/b42bc2f7b212eb288d2e7be289d251f15bfd.pdf.

scenes were hung on the wall or when plants were placed in hospital rooms.

The results of these studies prove that over the eons we, as a species, evolved to constantly interact with and always respond to nature in order to survive and thrive. These studies also show that our relatively recent withdrawal from nature over the decades is a proverbial "hard stop" for us as living creatures. Although this might be a swift and somewhat easy transition for the mind, that is not true for our bodies nor our spirit. The introduction of technology to many parts of the world in our current century has made us stop being active—which is what we are biologically evolved to be—and become very sedentary.

The lack of being in connection with our environment creates a form of sensory and spiritual deprivation that increases levels of anxiety, tension, and depression, to name only a few symptoms, others being much more severe.

These studies I shared make up only a tiny fraction of my hours of research that concludes that bringing nature in any form, into our everyday environments is a critical need for all of us. Based on this, I am firm in my personal belief that the techniques in this book, if applied properly, will significantly benefit you and your loved ones by increasing the potential for wellness in your daily lives. I will also offer suggestions on how to live more gently upon our planet, which will benefit the environment, animals, and people around the globe.

It doesn't mean that you have to be taking in the great outdoors by going on an expedition or long hike every day. You can receive benefits from bringing these elements into your home, sitting in a garden, or watching birds outside your window. Each of these elements creates positive effects that, although small in and of themselves, add up to major benefits and cultivate a sense of serenity.

I found that the practical application of basic Native American spiritual practices, when used in conjunction with responsible and mindful ways of using resources, produces a living space that does more than just benefit the people within it. It also reconnects you with nature. Renewing your interdependence with the natural world allows for you to be in sync with our Earth Mother and in turn makes you more sensitive to your own needs and the needs of others. Just like in times of old, paying attention to the climate around you, which is composed of the weather, the collective groups of people who are in your vicinity, and the energy of the land, will make you feel connected and grounded.

Being able to feel this current of sacred energy and the cycles of natural time will empower you. It gives you the ability to effortlessly move through your daily routines in a more relaxed manner. It also gives you the potential to more easily manifest what you wish to bring into your life. Why? Because you are cocreating in concert with what is being provided around you in real time versus becoming exhausted by constantly fighting the natural flow and imposing your will out of sync. Although we live in modern times, we are still children of Earth Mother. We are still sensitive to the changes of light, color, and the interactions between ourselves and nature just as all of our Ancestors were.

For those of you who have read my first book, *Journeying Between the Worlds,* some of the material is repeated here alongside many new exercises specific to this book, as these are important building blocks for using this method. The material explaining basic Native American spiritual concepts, fundamental exercises such as the Waterfall meditation and going on a

Medicine Walk, and the function of each element will seem very familiar.

However, I explain them a little differently in this book. I add more depth to their aspects and emphasize specific qualities that are necessary to understand so they can be applied practically when creating a happy home or work space using the Heart of the Earth method.

Two
Universal Native American Spiritual Principles

NATIVE AMERICAN SPIRITUAL principles evolved over time to be practical in addition to spiritual. Since each Nation lives in different climates and terrains, each developed unique traditions, teachings, and cultures that allow them to thrive in the lands where they live. Only the elders of that particular Nation have the right to choose with whom they share their wisdom. If ever you wish to learn the ways of a specific tribe, you must ask, respectfully, the elders of that Nation. However, the essence of certain teachings are universal and expressed in various forms regardless of where in the Americas you would travel. In order for you to have the full benefit of this book, you must understand these basic concepts.

GREAT SPIRIT
One of the names for the Creator spirit is the Great Spirit, although the One has countless names in many cultures. The

Creator is benign and is in all things and beyond all things. The Great Spirit is so vast it is impossible for us to be able to comprehend the complete nature of the Creator. All of us have the ability to connect with the Great Spirit at any time about anything by going into our Hearts. The teachings to help us live in harmony and balance with creation and with each other as a human family come from the Great Spirit.

It is said that all things come from and return to the Great Spirit. Since the Great Spirit is in all things and beyond all things, it is placed in the center of the Medicine Wheel. Because of this, the center of the Medicine Wheel is the most powerful point and spirit is the most powerful of all the five elements.

It is said that this divine force has allowed itself to be understood in many ways, nature being only one of them. In the Medicine Wheel, the Great Spirit has a male face that represents divine masculine force. This is represented by Sky Father. The Great Spirit also has a divine feminine face and represents all that is female, which is represented by Earth Mother. This element of spirit is invoked whenever there is a need to have different aspects or elements that are discordant work to come into alignment with each other.

It is also taught that the Great Spirit lives in our Hearts. This is why, when it comes to a location, the Heart is so important. It represents the breath and divine power of the Creator that will hold the essence, expression, and healthy sacred energy to govern and flow throughout an entire home or work space. Later in this book I will teach you how to carefully choose objects to place within the Heart of the space that you are working on.

Medicine Wheel

Although the Medicine Wheel is drawn as a circle with two intersecting lines it is more than merely a two-dimensional image. Just as we are more than beings who live in a three-dimensional world, the energy and effects of the Medicine Wheel go beyond this dimension to include the energetic and spiritual worlds and dimensions beyond our own. I would like for you to envision the Medicine Wheel similar to an atom. The position of the Great Spirit, which includes Earth Mother and Sky Father, would be considered the nucleus and axis of the atom.

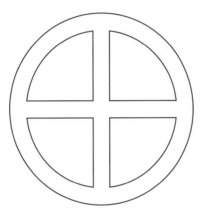

Figure 1: Medicine Wheel

Consider the compass points that are across from each other as defining the borders of the orbits that are moving around that nucleus. The center of this "atom," which is the place of the Great Spirit, carries the true Heart, or essence, of what you are trying to build. A hoop is created when two points opposite of each other on the Medicine Wheel are connected to create a circle around the center point, say, for example, east to west and back again, or southwest to northeast and back again. This hoop completes a circuit of energy that continuously flows back and forth. Each time it completes a circle it recharges the circuit. Even though the compass points are at opposite ends I do not want you to mistake them as conflicting forces.

As an illustration, I will use the hoop that goes from east to west and back again. Although in reality Earth is orbiting around the sun, I ask you to imagine the sun's movement across the sky as we perceive it. It appears in the east, tracks across the sky and sets in the west. Now, further envision the sun as it hides under the horizon, setting in the west to complete its cycle and rising back in the east again. From a spiritual standpoint the east represents birth and new beginnings, like the dawning of a new day moving forward into maturity, and outward expression as you move from east to west. The west represents going within yourself in order to truly understand what your life is about and who you are so that you can move forward, take a new perspective, and plan the next step into the next stage of your life. This is the flow of energy going from west to east.

This introduces the concept and energetic flow of sacred cycles, or Sacred Hoops, of Native American spiritualities. In this spiritual pathway it is taught that all things aspire to harmony. If you strive to increase harmony in your life, you need to take the time to understand the natural flow and rhythms of our magnificent Universe.

POWER

When Power is capitalized it means Breath of the Great Spirit. It is a divine neutral energy that is in all things and moves beyond all things. It brings life and vitality as well as the cycles of creation and destruction, life and death, renewal and release. This sacred energy is recognized and described in a similar fashion in other cultures as well. In Chinese culture it is known as *chi*, in Japanese culture it is known as *ki*, and in India it is known as *prana*. It is this sacred force that we respectfully harness when we manifest or let go of people or things in our lives.

HEART

The Heart is the place within you where you connect with the Creator, your Sacred Self and All Your Relations. Conscience, intuition, gut feelings, and emotions are some manifestations of Heart. It is capitalized to differentiate it from the physical organ in your body. This is the place within you where Power can be most easily felt and directed. It is also known as the Throne of the Soul. Within your physical body it would encompass the area from the throat to the solar plexus. Heart gives you the ability to communicate beyond words. It is through listening with your Heart that you will be able to correctly choose that which truly resonates in harmony with you to grow your greater good and promote your well-being.

ALL MY RELATIONS

It is taught that all things come from and return to the Breath of the Great Spirit. This Breath, this Power, is similar to the concept of *chi* or *prana*. Since all things in the creation come from this Breath, including us, it is said that all things and creatures of nature, seen and unseen, are All Our Relations. Humans are viewed as just another creation and *not* the pinnacle of it. It is said that we are no greater than the ants and no less than the mountains. We are spirits having a human experience, not humans having a spiritual experience.

SACRED HOOP

Native Americans observe the cyclical patterns of nature that strive to be in harmony. We see these patterns, or smaller hoops, in the waves of the ocean, the turning of the seasons, and the touching of generations. The interweaving of these cycles makes up the Sacred Hoop: it is both physical and spiritual and all of us are a part of it.

GOOD RED ROAD

Native American spiritualities, collectively called the Good Red Road, are earth-based spiritual paths. The Good Red Road is a way of life. It is connecting with the Breath of the Creator within us and around us that allows us to evolve with compassion as an individual soul and as a community of souls. Following the teachings of the Ancestors guides us to be good people and exist gently upon our Earth Mother by being ever mindful of the natural and spiritual worlds. We also acknowledge that the Creator gave each one of us an individual destiny as we try to reach our own dreams and goals.

As we strive to do all these things it creates a truly unique life path that is known as the Good Red Road. Even though we may seek guidance from teachers and helpers throughout the years, ultimately our life path is between us and the Great Spirit since no one else can completely comprehend our lives.

MEDICINE

The Breath of the Creator manifests within us as talents. Each one of us has a unique set of talents that are spiritual, physical, and mental, in addition to our personal way of being. When we apply these in a benign way, it is known as Good Medicine.

Since the Power of the Great Spirit moves through all things and beings of nature, everything has the potential of being Medicine. In order to make Medicine you need to harness Power, and how Medicine is applied determines whether it is Good Medicine, or Bad Medicine.

The Seven Arrows

The teachings say that there are seven sacred cardinal directions that are watched over by powerful divine spirits. They are known as the Seven Arrows. These sacred Beings maintain harmony and enforce the will of the Creator. Each of the Seven Arrows holds a unique energy, has specific teachings, and is associated with a particular element. As we go further in this book, I will teach you how to work properly with the Seven Arrows in relation to the Heart of the Earth method.

The Five Elements

Similar to several cultures around the world, many of the First Peoples also believe that everything is made of five elements. These elements are fire, air, water, earth, and, the greatest of them all, spirit. Each of these elements serves a different function in maintaining harmony and balance, and it is when these elements are out of balance that sickness, strife, and needless destruction occur. In the coming chapters I will go into greater detail about these elements and how to engage them to enrich your life.

Although this only scratches the surface of the teachings of the Good Red Road you have enough of an orientation for now. It is time to introduce fundamental principles that will put you in the proper frame of mind and Heart.

Three
ENERGETIC PRINCIPLES
AND FINDING YOUR CENTER

WE ARE MORE THAN just our physical body and the same can be said about our environment around us. Just as we can see the material world with our physical eyes, there is a part of our spirit that can keenly sense the energetic landscape that is present. The energetic landscape must be factored in as much as any physical concerns when building your space. As you begin to build your space in accordance with the Earth Mother it is paramount for you to understand these maxims.

LIFE IS BUT A DREAM
It has been said in various ways throughout the centuries that thoughts become things. This goes way beyond thoughts! When I was taught the sacred ways it was said that life was a dream. Life is merely the physical reflection of our aspirations, fears, hopes, and personal desires. This is true of each of us as individuals, and this impact on the world around us grows stronger exponentially as we dream collectively. A simple case where you can see this in

action is an apartment complex in which all the units have the same layout. When you open the door to each one you will find that each unit reflects a unique world that represents those who dwell within it. This idea applies within the building, the complex, the neighborhood, and so on. For the sake of simplicity, this book will focus solely on your personal space.

I mention this so that you may also be aware of the environment around you and how you affect it, and in turn how it affects you. Consider how our thoughts and our words color our perceptions of the world. The mind likes to create structure and where there is no structure the mind imposes its own. Structure is a fundamental human need that we use to get our bearings and try to make sense of the immense world speeding around us. If you see a half completed sketch of an animal, your mind will automatically fill in the lines. Another example is the common game of looking at clouds to see what form your mind and folly chooses it to have. As human beings we have the insatiable desire to turn the intangible and the untouchable into symbols and tangible things. It is why we like buying souvenirs, which are mementos of our experiences, and why we keep tokens of our loved ones, who have touched our lives, to keep them close to us.

CORE BELIEFS

I would like to give a teaching that was given to me during my journeys by the Bear Spirit. The Bear Spirit is a sacred spirit Being and teacher who assists people when they are doing profound inner work. The teaching is called Core Beliefs. It is made of two components. The first component is a belief. A belief is a conclusion we come to after an experience. If we keep having the same results after similar experiences, the stronger our belief becomes over time, and even more so over incarnations.

The second component is your Heart. As I mentioned before, your Heart spans the energetic spiritual centers from the throat to your solar plexus. It is where the Fire of the Creator lives within you. The Heart is where you connect to your own soul and to the greater whole. It is harnessing the divine Power found within your Heart that gives you the ability to create and to destroy. Combining the conviction of your beliefs with the Power of your Heart is what creates a Core Belief. Your Core Beliefs create a framework of energy that causes people and things to be attracted to you. It is *the* mechanism by which people, experiences, and ultimately what you will manifest come into your life. Whether you are conscious of it or not there are several Core Beliefs that act as lenses through which you see the world. It is necessary that you begin to understand your Core Beliefs for they will have an impact on your choices as to what feels right as you select what you want to put into the place that you are designing.

ATTITUDE

Attitude plays a critical role in how you interact with the world around you. If you wake up feeling well and with a good attitude, you tend to view the day as a positive one. Even if unpleasant things happen, it is easier to tolerate them and put them in a better light. Your attitude is another aspect of the energetic field you generate. It remains in any place you have spent time in. The more time spent in one place, the stronger the energetic impression that remains.

Consider it like spiritual scent marking. A good attitude creates positive, warm vibrations. If it were a scent, it would be like freshly baked bread or fresh flowers. A bad attitude creates negative, raw, and restless vibrations. If a bad attitude were an odor, it would smell like rotting meat or sickness. The emotions and attitude of others linger and can be felt as the ambience of a location. Your attitude is what people and your environment immediately respond to!

KEEP IT SHORT AND SIMPLE

Another hallmark of Native American spiritualities is that an act or ritual must be both practical and spiritual or it is not worth doing or having. By this I mean less is more! From a spiritual, energetic standpoint, having a few things you find beautiful and that nurture your spirit creates a base of healthy, sustaining energy. Keeping your place tidy allows for Power to smoothly flow around you.

From a practical standpoint, having fewer things makes a space that is a much easier to maintain. I am not saying that you have to be a minimalist! I am merely saying to choose possessions that truly serve you and, preferably, are low- to no-maintenance. That way you spend more time enjoying life instead of being a slave to taking care of a bunch of things. Having fewer things also allows for you to live simply so that others may simply live. The open space enables you to move freely, have a steady circulation of fresh air, and opens the path for the Breath of the Creator to flow easily. When you live comfortably, but not cluttered with needless material possessions, it permits others to have access to those resources so that they also may be able to enjoy the necessities of life.

CLOSING THE LOOP

In the Native American way of life you never take more than you can give and are always thinking about how to close the loop of an item. This means that before you buy an item, consider where it would go at the end of its life span with you. One simple example could be any technology you own. Thrown into a landfill, its poisonous chemicals would leach into the earth and groundwater as it *slowly* broke down over centuries. However, items like cell phones can be given to charities who refurbish them in order to help those who have need of them.

Consider the joy of not being married to things. It would stop the madness of endless consumerism. Many big companies try to impose upon you their "truth" that you are inadequate and always lack something. They try to make you believe that the more things you own the happier you will be. The illusion is that the more you spend (by giving them your money), this will somehow increase your sense of self-worth and will bring the admiration of others.

Employing the techniques of the Heart of the Earth helps to liberate you from these fictions by having you realize *you **are** enough.* Taking time to select a few special items that are meaningful, instead of a bunch of impulsive purchases, will make your rooms more spacious and give you a feeling of wellness that can enhance self-worth. This is much better than getting items for their own sake. The true value of what you place in your home lies in carefully choosing something that is a current and healthy expression of you and those you love.

Walking in Balance

Another key teaching is that of giving and receiving equally. Too often I run into people who give way more than they receive! Somehow the falsehood that states you should feel guilty for letting people know that you have needs as much they do is pandemic. Ultimately, this unrealistic belief creates exhaustion, resentment, conflict, and, potentially, burnout. Living your life with love, peace, kindness, and compassion for all beings means *including yourself in that equation.* When you feel healthy, calm, and content you are more capable of approaching all people and situations in your life with a clear mind and positive attitude. Walking in Balance should be practiced daily until it becomes second nature.

FUNCTION OF DUALITY: THE FORCES OF ORDER AND CHAOS

On the Good Red Road we also observe that this is a universe of dualities. This concept of dualities is repeated over and over again in our environment. Typically, these dual forces are equal but opposite in order to balance each other out. How we choose to employ them will determine whether these opposite energies will manifest as cooperation or conflict. Of these dual forces the pair that is universally relevant to us for the sake of this book is that of order and chaos.

The thought that order is good and chaos is bad is an opinion that is predominantly held in Western culture, but not exclusive to it. This is a natural preference because we, as human beings, like to have some form of structure so that we can orient ourselves in life. However, there must be balance.

In Native American spiritualities, order and chaos are seen as neutral and equally necessary forces. If something is overstructured, it ultimately becomes stagnant and will choke out the very spirit of why it was created. For example, it is not uncommon to have an agency in government be created to watch over the greater good of the community in response to a specific need. Over time it can develop so many rules and restrictions in order to protect itself that it no longer serves the people who created it in the first place.

Another example of this would be a family tradition that most people in that family would rather avoid. Year after year the family will come together reenacting a certain routine that everyone cannot wait to end. The reason that the tradition started was to bring joy and to create stronger family bonds. When that particular tradition becomes outdated but followed blindly with the idea of not wanting to anger or disappoint a member of the family, it becomes a tremendous bore, if not downright repellent. This also calls to mind people who are so strict in their expectations of how you should act or speak that a relationship with them becomes impossible. It is not long before we find ourselves resentful and rebellious to break free of these chain-like restrictions.

Too much chaos is a bad thing as well. I'm sure most of us have either witnessed a person or have struggled ourselves with living in eternal drama. In situations of nonstop drama, constant chaos follows and touches anyone who is unfortunate enough to permit themselves to be dragged into it. This can also happen when you have a series of events in your life that create one upheaval after the next. In those moments it's hard to tell which way is up or down. It can be extremely stressful because you do not know what to count on or what holds true. When things are in this state of upheaval nothing ever remains long enough to grow into something meaningful or act as a foundation to build on. Living this way makes us feel insecure and anxious.

So you see, the need to embrace both order and chaos as necessary but neutral is key to keeping a sense of stability. *There will always be chaos before new order.* I understand that chaos can be very frightening because it brings in the unknown and escorts out that which you find familiar. What you must remember is that anything that you truly value never really leaves you, but changes its form if you focus on it. This different form is the new order/structure that acts as a vehicle to help you to grow further on life's journey.

Let me use the simple idea of having fun to demonstrate this. When we were children our idea of having fun was very simple and very limited. The need to have fun in our lives never changes. But can you imagine having a rousing game of peekaboo with anyone beyond a toddler? Even then, because you are older this game becomes tiresome after a very short while. As you develop and have different life experiences, your concept of fun changes in relation to your tastes. The concept of fun can expand to lounging in a chair and staring at the stars on a beautiful night, reading an interesting book, having lively conversations, pursuing romance, or participating in an extreme sport.

The dynamics of duality is what helps to perpetuate change. If you participate with it, then chaos becomes purposeful and can even open the door to options and knowledge that you would not have seen or known before. With these new perspectives you can then consciously cocreate and manifest just about anything with the Universe. Mindfully applying what was unearthed by chaos creates fresh routines that, over time, become a lifestyle that reflect who you are today. These new structures and relationships, in turn, give a point of reference when you make choices as to what belongs in your life and what does not. These principles hold true in relation to what you physically manifest in a dorm, work space, or home.

My Chippewa-Ojibwe teachers taught that the forces of order and chaos move in a certain way along the Medicine Wheel. The way of order and building things up moves in harmony with the motion of the sun in the sky. This would be clockwise, or moving in a circle turning toward your right shoulder. This is the natural flow of energy of this physical world. The way of chaos or releasing, which we sometimes need to do when resetting energy, is moving against the sun, or counterclockwise. You would move in a circle turning toward your left shoulder.

For the vast majority of time you will always move sunwise (toward the right, in harmony). The reason being is the way of moving against the sun (toward the left, chaos) is a way of undoing. It is the natural flow of energy for the spirit realm. Moving against the sun is *never done lightly* and is performed only when there is a true need for it. It would be done in cases where something very bad or traumatic has happened or to release highly toxic energies or spirits. Even then, one would always finish with restoring the new order by moving the smoke or placing objects in a sunwise manner to resynchronize the flow of Power in harmony with the physical world. For all the techniques in this book you will only be moving in a sunwise direction.

THE ONLY CONSTANT IS CHANGE

When you are working on developing your space, do so with the idea that it will and should change over time. Remember your place is reflection of who you are and who you are becoming. Over the course of your life you will never stop evolving. As time goes by it is healthy to let go of the past, except for those few pieces that remain relevant.

For the most part no one likes change because of the fear of the unknown or because it is inconvenient. I would like you to reframe your thinking. The unknown brings wonderful possibilities. It is full of infinite potential. The unknown brings the gift of innovation and inspires creativity. The only way to get there is to go through brief periods of discomfort when you let go of what is familiar and focus on what you would like the next chapter of your life to be.

Yes, it can be a bit of a pain to create change. But consider this: Have you ever been to a place where everything is *very* outdated and the energy is *so* stagnant it can feel life-draining or claustrophobic? Remember that this is about you and the ones you love. You and your loved ones are worth it! The effort you put into this process is very satisfying because the result will be a home that is vibrant yet comfortable. When you keep thinking about the end result and how good your home or work space will feel, it will give you the motivation you need to keep on going.

GETTING IN TOUCH WITH YOURSELF AND ALL YOUR RELATIONS

One of the purposes of creating harmony within your home or work space is to have a sanctuary waiting for you where you can go at any time to comfortably be who you truly are. Your personal space is a place to recover, get grounded, become energized, center, and contemplate what is happening within yourself and your life. The spaces that you create using these techniques will reflect who you are, what is important to you, and where you are going in your life.

All too often I speak with people who are so caught up in their daily and work routines that they have lost touch with themselves and forgotten what makes them happy. This is compounded by a society that pressures us to present a persona that is "acceptable." In order to craft a space that is as unique as you are, you need to embrace yourself. Take a moment to contemplate what makes you feel happy and content. If you find that you are at a loss, make time to discover what these things are.

Engage in activities that are interesting to you or that you are curious about and break the rut you are stuck in. Don't be surprised if suddenly you feel self-conscious or guilty about your sense of self-worth. Unless you are shirking your responsibilities or acting unethically, this unfounded guilt is an old belief that you have dragged along with you through the years and it does not serve you!

If you are still having a tough time in allowing yourself to receive, then ask this question: Would you deny this source of self-nourishment to someone you love? If the answer is no, then you should not deny yourself either. Learn to care for yourself as much as you care for someone whom you deeply love. Listening to your inner child will help you go far in learning about yourself and rekindling a sense of wonder as you explore the world around you.

⋙ Exercise ⋘
Reconnecting with Your Inner Child

Reconnecting with your inner child is easier than you might expect. This simple exercise will take about ten to twenty minutes. Make sure to bring a pen and a piece of paper or, better yet, a journal, to write down your thoughts. Go to a place where you feel safe and you won't be disturbed. Don't forget to silence your electronics.

Think back to a happy event in your childhood where you experienced a sense of wonder or excitement. Relive that moment and focus on the details of it. Reconnect with those blissful emotions and what created them. Allow for these good feelings to fill every part of your body and Heart. Write down your observations. I sometimes find it useful to audio record them so that the inflections of my voice that hold the subtleties of my emotions are also captured.

Holding on to these feelings, reflect on what currently re-creates them or things that you would like to try that inspire these warm feelings within you. You should be able to recognize what truly gives you joy in your very being because the person, item, or event will produce the same feelings in your body and Heart as the joyful event that your childhood memory did.

Seeing your life through the eyes of your happy inner child will be like seeing the world with new eyes again. This can be especially healing if you've come from a background that was judgmental, domineering, or toxic. Giving yourself permission to just be yourself is incredibly empowering! You will find yourself eager to discover different forms of self-expression.

Approaching yourself with openness while leaving behind negative self-talk and harsh judgment is incredibly liberating. Do not be so quick to try to settle down into another routine. Instead, enjoy this time of freedom that you are gifting yourself. The idea is to get out of a box not entirely of your making, and to not rush putting yourself into another one.

FINDING YOUR CENTER

The greater part of working with the Heart of the Earth technique is being able to find your own center. Too many times people try to find happiness outside of themselves and ultimately end up being frustrated and disillusioned. One of the maxims of the Bear Spirit says, "Work with your nature and not against it." In order to know what you need to create for your well-being, you must understand yourself better. It is paramount not to be nitpicky nor negatively critical about yourself during this process, for those negative feelings will merely act as a distraction and keep you from your goal. You need to embrace yourself for who you are and from that choose what you need in order to thrive.

I know that sometimes this can be difficult. Too many times we weigh ourselves against standards that are a combination of culture, experiences throughout our childhood, or things we are taught during our school years. See how many of those standards truly apply to who you are today. Even if you agree with the values, make sure how you express them is authentically yours and not something that is done by rote. Remember that these influences do more than impact your beliefs and how you perceive the world. They can affect how you present yourself to others, causing you to stifle self-expression and needlessly limit your tastes, which in turn will impact how you craft your space.

☙ EXERCISE ❧
REFLECTING ON HAPPINESS

An exercise that may be useful is to think of a belief that you have about happiness. Reflect on where this belief came from. Is it truly something that makes *you* happy? Or is it something you were told that is *supposed* to make you happy? Does it allow for you to feel contentment in solitude or with others? Do you deny yourself a healthy expression of your joy because you are afraid of the criticism of others? If so, why? If a particular expression of happiness seems forced in any way, or if you have lost track of what makes you happy, then you must begin to explore why you are holding on to this belief or why are you keeping yourself in this state.

You will know when a belief is yours when it truly resonates within your own Heart *and* it makes sense within your own mind. It is useful to repeat this contemplation with different things that you hold true. Since you will be connecting with Earth Mother and All Your Relations while using the Heart of the Earth method, you will have to do this reflective exercise so that you can articulate what your beliefs are regarding nature before you proceed further with this book.

Another critical step is to be able to listen to your own Heart. This is a foundational piece you need to understand in order to have success. Heart is not emotions. Emotions are merely one of the expressions of Heart. Heart is where the Breath of the Creator resides within you. It is where the essence of your being exists. It is the part within you that always knows and is never wrong, similarly described as "feeling it in your bones."

Your Heart is the quiet place that lies between the chattering of the mind and the waves of emotions. This is the place within you that helps you feel connected to All That Is when you exhale with contentment on a beautiful spring day. It is the place of peace within you that is always there regardless of whether you connect with it or not. I will provide you tips to help you discern when your Heart is speaking to you versus your mind. Your Heart and mind need to work in concert when crafting your space.

TIPS: DISCERNING WHEN THE HEART OR MIND IS SPEAKING

Determining whether the Heart or mind is speaking is something that we do so naturally that we take it for granted. Being able to tell the difference between whether your Heart or your mind is speaking to you is a very useful tool. If something is being generated initially from your Heart, then it will have a resonance that will move through you. There's a strong sense of conviction and/or emotions attached to it. It is not uncommon for your mind to need to catch up to your Heart and to take time to think it through to find words or ways to convey what the Heart is expressing. When your mind misinterprets what your Heart is trying to tell you, you will have a feeling that you are incorrect and you have to keep on searching for the right words.

If something is initially generated from your mind, you will be able to identify your line of reasoning, or at the very least be able to trace where those thoughts came from. Thoughts are easily molded to conform to your emotions or the situation as you perceive it. Since your mind likes to find structure in all things, its tendency will be to correlate causes and effects.

However, if your Heart and your mind are at odds, your first reflex might be to squash one or the other. This is unfortunate since both have something equally valid to say. Listen to each, accurately articulate what your Heart and mind are trying to say, then find a compromise between them.

If your Heart and your mind are of an accord, then whatever you are contemplating will feel right from a deeper sense. However, it might be difficult to discern where your thoughts originated from. In crafting your space it is important that both your Heart and mind agree. If you design a room for work that your mind deems efficient but your Heart does not feel warmth from it, the space will become increasingly difficult to remain in while getting things done. Ultimately, you will find yourself spending less and less time there, perhaps even abandoning the space altogether.

If you design a room for creativity that your Heart feels is perfect but your mind was not allowed to give input on, then you will end up with an impractical space that is chaotic. In the end you will abandon this room because it will become cluttered and not conducive to starting anything, much less finishing it.

Current society praises those people who work and act like machines. Machines do not have emotions, nor basic needs like resting and friendship. Unlike people, they have no need to exist other than for the functions they are fabricated to perform. You are not a machine! *Kindness to self begins with embracing your own humanity.* It is by practicing compassion to yourself that you can begin to extend compassion empathetically to other living beings, which is a prerequisite for working with the Heart of the Earth method. I teach that what you do to the Earth Mother you do to yourself, and what you do to yourself you do to the Earth Mother. This is another small hoop of life and, from my viewpoint, a cardinal principle to live by.

Living Mindfully to Reconnect with Earth Mother

Part of reconnecting with Earth Mother is to live your life mindfully. There are several ways to accomplish this. One way is being thoughtful of yourself and others by practicing common courtesies so that there can be greater harmony wherever you are. Common courtesy increases goodwill. It lessens the pollution of negative energy into the environment. Another example of being mindful is practicing random acts of kindness and compassion. This doesn't have to be limited to just human beings, it's good to practice compassion to all living things. In modern times, this idea includes purchasing products that are fair trade and cruelty free, not putting substances down the drain that would poison our waters, and supporting sustainable practices for our planet. The list could go on and on.

Although it would be unrealistic to expect all people to respond in this same manner, All Your Relations in nature will notice. On a personal level, you might find that the Universe is responding by making it easier for you to find what you need in order to lead a more fulfilling and joyous life. On a grander scale, the generations of the future will have a brighter world to live in because you took the time to care.

Another basic rule for living mindfully is to never take more than you can give. This runs opposite of the current philosophy of materialism that is prevalent in our society. A good illustration of this philosophy in action are paper companies that follow the practices of processing paper without toxic chemicals and replanting trees to replace the ones harvested for paper. Part of Walking in this tradition means adopting a lifestyle that promotes sustainability for our planet.

SAGE VERSUS WARRIOR

One of the ways to begin connecting with your Heart is through meditation. There are two forms of meditation, the Way of the Sage and the Way of the Warrior. The Sage's way to meditate is through quiet contemplation while being still. The Warrior's way is through focused movement that engages the mind and body, which allows the person's spirit and mind to be more open to all that is around them. Both are equally valid methods to develop your skill to meditate. Although it is natural to have a preference for either the Sage's way or the Warrior's way, idealistically it will make you more balanced and give you more flexibility to be able to do both methods.

✐ EXERCISE ✐
WAY OF THE SAGE—WATERFALL MEDITATION

One exercise I will share with you so that you may meditate like a Sage is the Waterfall meditation. To begin, find a place that is comfortable and relaxing for you. I would ask that for the duration of this time, you turn off all electronic devices that may distract you. Sit with your feet flat on the floor and in an upright position. Close your eyes and focus on your breathing. Focus on how your breath feels as it moves over your breastbone. Realize that this is the Breath of the Creator that moves through you and connects you with the Great Spirit and All Your Relations.

Relax every muscle in your body, from your eyes, the corners of your mouth, your arms, all the way down to your fingertips. Soften your belly and your back, and loosen every muscle in your legs down to the tips of your toes. *Take your time.* Allow for that wave of relaxation to move through you. Focus on feeling the energy of the Earth Mother beneath your feet. Draw that sacred Power through the soles of your feet and up your legs, filling your body, your arms to your fingertips, up to your neck, and through the crown of your head.

This sacred energy on its own will continue to flow up to Sky Father and He will return it back to Earth Mother. With every breath, with every heartbeat, allow yourself to be in this sacred flow of energy so that it fills every cell in your body. It will clear your mind, strengthen your Heart, and rejuvenate your body. As you listen to your heart beating, feel how the sacred Power fills your Heart and connects you with the Creator and to All Your Relations.

This exercise is called the Waterfall because it teaches how the Power flows through all things and creates a Sacred Hoop, very much like the cycle of water. Water comes up from underneath the earth to find the surface, evaporates, goes up to the sky, condenses, and comes back down to the earth. It is the never-ending cycle that has kept our beautiful planet alive for eons. Breathing is another example of a Sacred Hoop. When you inhale you are receiving Power; when you exhale you are giving back to it, which honors the sacred precept of giving and receiving equally.

Visit my website listed in the resources secti
to purchase the audio support for this medit

❧ EXERCISE ☙
WAY OF THE WARRIOR—MED

The easiest way to meditate for most people is to use the Way
of the Warrior. You may even have meditated this way without
knowing it! The Way of the Warrior method involves both the
body and mind being engaged in a repetitive but relaxed activity that requires minimal mental concentration. It allows for you
to be open and receptive to what your Heart has to say. This is
why most people get their best ideas and insights when they are
driving, doing basic chores, or relaxing as they read a book. This
same method is used in disciplines of meditating like martial arts
and yoga.

A technique to meditate like a Warrior is to go on a Medicine
Walk. For this exercise you will be going for a walk outside. It
doesn't matter if it's a local park, a walking path at work, or a
nature trail. Make sure to give yourself at least twenty minutes
so you are not rushed. It is preferable that you turn off all electronic devices for the duration of this exercise, or at the very least
silence them. Pick a day when you feel the weather is beautiful—
it does not have to be a sunny day. Any day you enjoy will do. I
personally know people who truly enjoy rainy days, windy days,
and snowy days.

Make sure that you are dressed appropriately and comfortably for the climate that you will be walking in. You will find that
it is easier for you to be successful with this exercise if you go to
a place where there are not too many people. However, safety and
common sense always come first. *Never* walk in a place that is too

ate, where you can put yourself at risk for harm or have an ccident because the terrain is too tricky.

First, loosen up by stretching. It does not need to be a formal routine. Briefly standing tall and with your arms outstretched is sufficient. A good yawn helps too! Observe your environment. Let your eyes take in the beauty of our Earth Mother and Sky Father. Focus on your physical senses. Notice how your ears hear the sounds of life around you. Your nose and tongue smell and taste the scents that are on the air. Take in the sights all around you. Pay attention to how your body feels and how it is connecting to where you are. Be completely in the moment. Nothing else exists but now. Drop your shoulders and breathe deeply.

Once you feel that you are in the moment, begin walking. As you walk, stay present and let your senses connect you with All Your Relations. Let your breath, heartbeat, and the cadence of your footsteps help you stay rooted, but keep your consciousness flowing as it connects with the present moment. Let your mind and your Heart be open. Acknowledge any thoughts or emotions that begin to surface, but let them move through you like a gentle breeze. Do *not* hold on to them!

If you find that you fall out of being completely present, do not focus on it. Simply stop walking and fully reconnect with your senses as you did before. Being distracted is normal, but will become less frequent as you grow into this practice. You may use this as a mantra if you need to: "All that exists now is my breath [focus on your breath], my heartbeat [focus on your heartbeat], my footsteps [feel and hear the rhythm of your footfalls], and feeling the connection between myself and nature [be aware of what is around you]."

When you feel this flow, you are allowing yourself to feel Power, which is the Breath of the Creator, and being in oneness with the Great Spirit and All Your Relations. When you are done with your walk, stop, close your eyes, and give thanks to the Creator and All Your Relations. You know you have done this properly when, even after you are done with your walk, you still can feel that sacred flow of Power filling your Heart, moving through you and around you.

You should try this exercise while walking through familiar surroundings. As you go through your day, pay attention to how some of your surroundings will feel very welcoming and comforting, while others will feel tense or foreboding. Take time to observe the details as to why these locations create these feelings in you. It is preferable that you physically visit these places, if you can, instead of just thinking about these locations. Sometimes when we visit the extremes of our spectrum of personal tastes, it helps us to find the comfortable middle point. I recommend taking notes on these walks because if you find any consistent patterns of an environment that makes you feel happy and safe, you will want to try to replicate this in some fashion in your space.

For myself, I realized that I felt the most comfortable walking through a park, in a verdant atrium, or any place that had houseplants. In short, for a place to feel like home to me, there needs to be at least one living green plant of some sort. I also observed that I prefer places that have bright colors, rather than neutral or dark colors, because to me they feel more alive and inviting. Ideally you should be able to meditate equally well as a Sage and Warrior, so practice both techniques routinely. However, it is normal to have a natural predisposition to one over the other.

THE FIVE ELEMENTS

We will now look at the five elements and the functions they perform. It is through their interplay that all that we see around us is in existence. How the elements are interacting together determines whether a place will be harmonious or discordant. By being able to identify the five elements, how they interact with each other, and the effect they have within your environment, you will be able to work with them to design the space that is perfect for you.

Fire: The Life Spark of Energy Found in All Things

The element of fire represents the Power of the Great Spirit that gives life and is one of the most dynamic of elements. Fire is the element of the life force itself found running through all of creation. It is very much like a living being. It needs to be brought into life by the production of a single spark or ember. Fire also needs to be nurtured, protected, and fed much like an infant, so it can grow from infancy, to childhood, and into adulthood. It needs to eat and have air in order to survive. When a fire is left unattended, it ages, reduces, and eventually dies. Fire is the element of bringing things to life.

When fire is in balance and under control, it illuminates, brings warmth, and provides the energy for one thing to become another, like turning raw ingredients into a cooked meal. When it is out of control, it rages like a firestorm and destroys beyond recognition all that it touches. It is the element of powerful transformation.

Air: The Winds of Communication and Travel

Air is the element that represents thought and process. Just as sound travels through air, air carries our words, which are expressions of our thoughts. Air also represents communication. When the air is clear, we can breathe. We use the expression of clearing the air when we have resolved a misunderstanding. Air represents how our minds seek to create structure and meaning in our lives, and in the natural world around us. It is one of the fastest moving of elements and it represents swift movement and travel.

When air is in balance it sustains life and allows for steady communications, whether it be remotely or in person. When air is out of balance, it devastates like a tornado. Everything becomes choked and cloudy; clear thought and relaying of messages is impossible. The lack of balance can also cause projects and relationships to become destroyed through thoughts that are either too broad or too narrow.

Water: The Element of Heart and Unity

The element of water is the element of Heart. It is symbolic of our emotions and our intuitions, which are expressions of Heart. Water is a symbol of unity. Indeed, our planet is a water planet and our bodies are mostly made of water. It is the element of water that helps us express what words cannot. This is the element that is used to share our dreams and hopes at a soul level. Water is the element of the empath.

When water is in balance, it helps us to connect with our own inner knowing, share healthy love in all its forms, and build stable communities. Just as water can wash away any dirt on our bodies, this spiritual element purifies us so that we can be refreshed and rejuvenated. When water is out of balance, it rages and roars like a hurricane destroying all in its path, getting its power from blind emotions or fears. It will drown out reason and our ability to hear the voice of the Great Spirit within us.

Earth: The Element of Stability, Foundations, and Building

Earth is the slowest moving but the longest lasting of the elements. The only element that endures longer than earth is spirit. Earth represents our physical bodies, the environment around us, and the items within them. Earth creates solid foundations, like the foundations of a building. It is this element that allows us to create symbolic images of the intangible to make it tangible. Earth represents prosperity, shelter, and determination. This is the element that will be used to help you manifest what you need into physical form and hold the energy of your space in a stable way.

When earth is in balance, it helps to set the steady rhythm of your life and provides you with the raw materials to bring your dreams and aspirations into reality. When earth is out of balance, it levels everything beyond recognition, like an earthquake that shakes everything apart.

Spirit: The Universal Element and Transcendence

The greatest element of all is spirit because it is the purest representation of the Creator. It is *the* element that is found in all things and beyond all things. Spirit helps us to transcend ordinary daily life. It rejuvenates and heals all that it touches. Although it is the most difficult element to understand, it is the most important to meditate upon. Spirit restores all things to their proper place and path and allows our souls to understand universal divine law.

Spirit is the element that we use to harness the other elements. It indicates how to properly express what we want to attract into our lives in a sustainable way and bring into being what we truly value. Spirit is forever in harmony and does not suffer being misused. It brings what we have earned from karma into the physical world, restoring balance to all that it touches.

When these five elements are in balance, our lives will feel complete and run in a healthy manner that feels normal to us. It is when the elements are out of balance that they can create difficulties or sickness. Say, for example, you have an area of your home that is very cluttered. It is littered with items from your past to the point where your living space is completely stagnant. Here we would say the elements of earth (the clutter) and water (sentimental objects from the past that are no longer relevant in the present) are out of balance. The other three elements must be employed before correcting earth and water directly.

Imagine this scenario being like a set of scales where earth and water are tipping the scales out of balance. Adding the other three elements—fire, air, and spirit—into the other bowl of the scale helps to restore balance. In this particular case, the element of fire would help to highlight what would bring novel energy and what type of energy is needed to bring new life and vitality.

The element of air, representing thought, creates a plan to sort what items are still useful and what to give away. Air will find a way to organize the items that remain. It can also introduce a new philosophy or mindset that would help to create a spark to grow.

Spirit puts the entire situation into proper focus. This element will point out the patterns of how the situation got to this level and what is needed to have it move on in a healthy way. Spirit gives insight into important memories and lessons of the past, what needs to be learned, and points out new behaviors needed to make for a better future. It will guide air and fire in regards to how much of each element will be used to clear the way. Clarity on how to proceed with these three elements will produce a plan with clear steps on how to resolve the problem.

With a clear plan, only then can earth be tackled with the objects physically being sorted through to decide what to keep and what to give way. Water, in this scenario, can finally attain a healthy level when going through these items because the emotions the items hold can finally be processed. The individual would finally be at peace to give these possessions away and reduce the clutter. If needed, water enables healing from grief or reliving happy memories of the past. It opens the Heart to thinking how these joys can be expressed in a different way in the future.

HOW THE ELEMENTS AFFECT EACH OTHER

When the elements are interacting with each other, they create active forces that bring movement and change. The interaction of the elements is not only amongst the cardinal points themselves, but with the points between them, otherwise known as the Walking Winds.

It is important to have a working understanding of these concepts. This information will come into play in chapter 7 when you are creating your space and establishing the dominant energy by choosing items or colors that represent the element within a room in relation to which compass point the space is facing. For now, I would like you to envision how these elements interact with each other in the natural world, which will make it much easier to intuitively understand their energies and what they feel or look like when translated into your daily experiences.

Interaction of the Elements among the Four Cardinal Points

The elements that are opposite of each other require the utmost care when interacting with each other, but, if successful, produce powerful forces that are stable and reliable. On the Medicine Wheel, elements that are opposite provide teaching energy and completion to each other. Yes it can be a challenge, but once you have mastered the interplay of the elements you can build solid foundations.

It's important to understand that mastering a challenging energy is something that does not come easily, but is worthwhile to learn. Doing so will give you tremendous fulfillment, flexibility, and a sense of confidence. As you read on, I will teach you how to engage with a challenging energy whenever it arises so that it becomes a complementary force instead of an opposing one. These are the Sacred Hoops that you want to master and engage for any project or relationship that you want to last long-term. When out of balance, the elements will cancel each other out or create endless turmoil in the fight for trying to be the dominant element.

East and West

The elements of fire (east) and water (west) combined bring life to the Heart. The element of fire helps to illuminate possibilities that the Heart may be seeking to create beautiful manifestations and meaningful relationships. The compassion of Heart, found in the element of water, helps to temper the transformational essence of fire. When harnessed properly, the combination of fire and water produces steam, which creates the energy to move things forward in a powerful and steady way. In history, the invention of the steam engine brought on the industrial revolution. When out of balance, these two elements will escalate in their rage and passions until one or the other is either snuffed out or burned away.

North and South

The combination of elements of earth (north) and air (south) can be very awe-inspiring. When in balance and properly harnessed, the effects of earth and air can be summed up in the phrase "thoughts become things." Out of all the combinations of elements, the combination of earth and air can be the most laborious and painstaking, but the energy created out of it can last for centuries. Both of these elements require attention to detail and observing cause and effect. This is the combination you want to use for creating bridges between generations, people, concepts, and nations. The feeling of this combination of earth and air is one of determination and participating with mindful compassion for the greater good of yourself and others. When out of balance, these elements become stubborn, and in their fight for supremacy, will blow away or crush beyond recognition anyone or anything that stands in their path.

The Interaction of the Elements Within the Walking Winds

As mentioned before, the points between, or the Walking Winds, hold dynamic energy that is extremely powerful. There are many benefits in using these intense forces. But, they are like the heat found in a ghost pepper: a little bit can go a very long way! One of the benefits is being able to move extremely stagnant energy, which allows for there to be a breath of fresh air so that the flow of life can break through.

The Walking Winds are the mover and remover of obstacles. An example of this aspect is facilitating healing from trauma. The Walking Winds ease suffering because they release people who are frozen in time reliving events of extreme grief or some major tragedy. The Winds escort people to a place of recovery to restore a healthy life. The power of these forces is strong enough to break the chains of generational abuse. The Winds also help to reframe things so that a new look on life can be harnessed. This new perspective directs a person's actions so that a totally new lifestyle can be achieved.

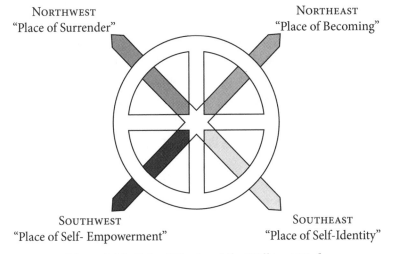

NORTHWEST
"Place of Surrender"

NORTHEAST
"Place of Becoming"

SOUTHWEST
"Place of Self- Empowerment"

SOUTHEAST
"Place of Self-Identity"

Figure 2: Medicine Wheel and the Walking Winds

The Walking Winds can do more than just move stagnant energy. They can actually reset the energy of a place. This is especially good if things, projects, or people fall into misalignment from their original intentions, which in turn ends up in needless or even extreme destructive chaos. The most common occurrences of this are when romantic relationships fall apart or business partnerships become combative and dissolve. Here the proper use of the Walking Winds can help to seed an energy in a location so that manifestations can take place as originally intended.

These forces also have the ability to create deep cleansing and clearing of any location. This can be used when a site has been the scene of some horrific and/or criminal act. In this case, the points between help to scour clean any residue from these horrible events so that the area returns to its original baseline of energy in its pure, pristine state.

Finally, the Walking Winds, because of their intense catalytic properties, can actually jump-start your environment. Imagine a place that feels devoid of life or has no moving energy at all. Using the Walking Winds is very much like putting the electric paddles of a defibrillator to a heart that has stopped and jolting it to begin beating again. The energy of the points between also assists if things are slowing down or becoming erratic. The energy of these directions can help to ensure that the natural rhythms of a location are reinstated so that life can return to being normal or even better than before.

COMBINED ELEMENTS

By now you are becoming familiar with the concept that all things have an expression that manifests when they are in balance and when they are out of balance. I would like to go further explaining the variations that happen with the Walking Winds.

Elements of the Northeast

The combination of fire (east) and earth (north) is very useful when there is the need to reboot the energy of a place. The combination of these two elements, when working together properly, brings about endless ideas and how to properly manifest them. This is a perfect energy when trying to engage a community or a team to accomplish goals bigger than they ever have before. It brings joy of enthusiasm with the rewards of accomplishment.

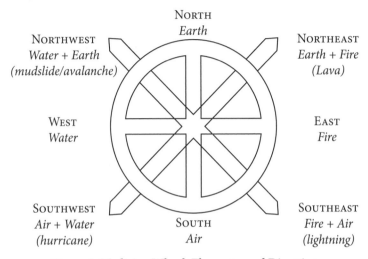

Figure 3: Medicine Wheel, Elements, and Direction

When out of balance, one can imagine these two elements combined together as lava with the tendency to melt everything down indiscriminately. When out of balance, the combination of the elements of earth and fire, north and east, can be personified as someone who misguides or misinforms other people in order to exploit them. A sad example of this would be when people are thinking that they are donating to a charity after a disaster only to find out that the organization was a fraud and that their money was wrongfully taken from them.

Elements of the Southeast

The combination of fire (east) and air (south) is one of the most unpredictable and quick of the catalytic forces, so this combination must be used sparingly and for brief periods only! The elements of the southeast require steady discipline and laser focus to keep in balance because they know no bounds. When in balance, these elements combine to form the power of lightning itself. The impossible becomes possible! The combination of fire and air, when in balance, helps to elevate the energy of a place, project, or relationship. If engaged for spiritual practices, these elements greatly ease the pursuit of enlightenment.

Another application for the elements of the southeast would be overcoming procrastination by restoring the balance between how to properly look at life and effectively engaging with life's energies and resources. In this form, everything that this lightning touches comes to life and anything seems reasonable, even if it is folly. This combination of elements, if carefully used, is perfect for elevating causes, cementing bonds within a community or a movement, or putting magic back into any tired relationship. The elements of the southeast are the ones you want to use when you wish to regain lost time. However, the amount of energy you might need to use to keep up with the pace of lightning could easily burn you out.

When these elements are combined and out of balance, it will seem that nothing can prosper. Things will manifest at an unnaturally high rate of speed and not as you intended. When the elements of the southeast are out of balance, they can also cause things to quickly fall apart in chaos. Burnout will be very common. Exhaustion and arguments will become prevalent. The elements of the southeast have no grounding force, so when they are out of balance, these elements will create a flash in the pan effect. In heated emotional situations, the imbalance can escalate things rapidly out of control until they become churned into a dangerous fury.

Elements of the Southwest

The combination of air (south) and water (west) is one that will have deep and long reaching effects for many years. A physical example of this combination is the creation of the Grand Canyon, the result of wind and water working in concert through the centuries. When in balance, the combination of air and water helps to strengthen the connection between head and Heart. The balance of these two elements helps to create an environment that can deepen the bonds between people. It is also one that allows for a more profound communion to be held between oneself, nature, and with the realm of the spirits. The well-balanced combination of these two elements can bring tremendous healing, especially to long-term problems such as overcoming addictions, PTSD, or breaking the chains of generational abuse. The combination of these two elements reinforces focus and steady commitment.

When these two forces are out of alignment, they produce the destructive power of a hurricane. The elements of the southwest can greatly exacerbate an argument between the head and the Heart. A person can feel as if they are caught up in the unending churning between scattered mental chatter and emotional unrest. This type of environment creates anxiety and feelings of desperation, leaving one to question if they can survive and keep their head above water.

Elements of the Northwest

The final combination of the Walking Winds would be that of earth (north) and water (west). This is an extremely beneficial coupling for fertility in all of its forms. This combination represents the speaking of one's dreams and desires of the Heart and the ability to convert them into reachable goals through the execution of practical plans. The combination of earth and water, north and west, helps to bring long-term manifestations that are satisfying and built upon sturdy and stable foundations.

The energy of the northwest is employed when you are trying to create balance within yourself and in your lifestyle. The most common challenge that northwest energy could be used for would be balancing time for one's own personal needs, the demands of work, and the responsibilities of family and household. The combination of north and west helps to make sure that all of your responsibilities are properly taken care of and that you are not lost within that equation.

When water and earth are out of balance, the imbalance produces terrible results with the force of an avalanche. Examples of this imbalance can be seen when relationships or situations are suddenly and sometimes violently wiped out. The imbalance can be seen as a combination of irrational emotions that drive the impulsive execution of radical (and often disastrous) "solutions." These are the forces that bring about war and create grievous wounds within a society, such as racism, that can harm future generations.

Whenever you have the Walking Winds interacting with each other, such as the northeast interacting with the southwest, they will automatically put themselves into balance when the element of spirit is added. All five elements will be represented at that point with spirit being the one that oversees them all.

When an Element
Is Represented More Than Once

When an element is represented more than once in a room, the benefits and detriments of that element are magnified accordingly. In the next chapter I will explain the function of each room and the element it represents, but for now it is more important to understand the mechanics of this process. If a room is located in the north, which holds the element of earth, and the room being created is a workshop, which also represents the element of earth, then the advantages and difficulties of this element would manifest twofold.

When you wish to lessen the effect of a duplicated element, you must introduce the element that is opposite to it on the compass. In this scenario of creating a workshop in a northern room, there is no harm in leaving the room as is, but if you would like to even it out, you would need to introduce the element of air. This would have to be done in two ways, such as having a device to play music while you work and books or videos to inspire creativity. If you would like the room to have a slightly heavier bend toward the element of earth, then the element of air would only need to be introduced once by using just music or just books.

Four
THE LAY OF THE LAND
❦

THIS CHAPTER DISCUSSES what is to be considered when analyzing the part of your home or land you wish to rebalance.

DISCERNING THE MAKEUP OF YOUR ENVIRONMENT

In analyzing a location so that you may use the Heart of the Earth method to make a space your own, you have to understand the topography of the space around you from both a physical and energetic point of view. This is a similar idea that an architect or engineer uses when they survey the land and its features before constructing a building. The survey makes sure that the land is appropriate for the building's function and that the building will be able to endure the environment that it is built in. However, the Heart of the Earth method differs in that it is not trying to dominate or to dramatically alter the land, but is working in concert with the topography of the surroundings you are in.

Upon observing the land, you will notice that it has many features. Some are physical and some are energetic. Carefully observing all the different aspects of a place can tell you whether it is a good fit for you. This idea applies even if you are already dwelling or working in a space and have to discover what is needed to increase the flow of harmony and to diminish areas that are counterproductive.

The ambient energy for a man-made space can be perceived by the architecture of a building, how a room is designed, and where it is located. Keep in mind that you must include the other underlying spiritual components of a location, which is to factor in all beings seen and unseen that exist within it. Only then will your assessment be complete. This is where you need to listen not only with all of your five senses, but your own Heart. It is the intangible essence that causes you to resonate with a place or feel repelled by it.

In Native American spiritualities, the practice of working in harmony with our environment is omnipresent. Working in cooperation with the land enhances what we are building. You need to pay attention to the overall geography and climate of the area you are in. Observe the man-made features and the type of buildings that are in your vicinity and the functions they are supposed to serve. Pay attention to the living beings upon the land—the people, animals, and plants. Does the environment look healthy? Are the buildings and people upon it in harmony with one another or do things seem incongruous and tense? Is the community and neighborhood well planned and have they taken the local ecology into account?

It is very useful to have a general understanding of the history of the area and community that you are considering living in. Since the Heart, which is the essence of the land, has a specific energetic frequency, you will find that if you dig further into the history of a place, whether it a region or of a particular home, there will be certain themes that repeat over and over again.

As I have stated before, the land has a Heart of its own. There are places where the natural world can feel welcoming and other places where it can feel foreboding. What one may define as the ambience of a space is actually the use of instincts to accurately define the disposition of the space. You might experience this feeling when you go to a place multiple times and sometimes get a good feeling and other times an unhappy one. Land attracts people who resonate with its own energy and if a person builds on it in accordance to what the land is asking, they will find that their life is rich and extremely fulfilling. However, if someone goes against the energy of a place, they will find themselves plagued with problems and struggling to prosper.

In Native American traditions, we acknowledge that there are nonphysical beings that have always resided upon the land and in the natural world. Are there spirit beings present where you are attempting to build a harmonized space? If so, what type are they? In addition to this, pay attention to see if the innate energy of the land beneath you is agreeable to what you are trying to achieve. If the land is one that likes to attract new life to itself, then an edifice such as a warehouse, which is meant to keep things stagnant, would be repelled by the Heart of the land. However, this same land would be very welcoming to spaces that generate feelings of unity, growing families, creativity, and prosperity for all.

PHYSICAL FEATURES

Some of the most obvious features of the land will be the physical aspects. Observing the topography, the water features, and the beings and creatures that dwell at a specific location can give you profound insights as to what the land welcomes. Of course, everything is in relation to itself.

Say, for example, an area that normally was composed of fields was suddenly dug up for a quarry, disfiguring the land. This will generate a harsh and potentially wounded vibe that will affect everything within that immediate region. However, if you are in the mountains where the natural topography is one of steep cliffs and jagged stones or littered with boulders, then you will find it is much easier spiritually to connect with the land and to find profound peace there. This is true wherever the natural topography has not been disturbed. Remember, too, that nature prefers Power to flow gently. It manifests as wind and water flowing over sharp angles, and over time, rocks become smooth, like tumbled river stones.

NATURAL FEATURES

Since I like to keep things simple, I am going to break down some basic natural components that need to be considered when determining the Heart of a region.

Flatlands to Mountains

A place that is level can hold Power steadily, but can also be prone to inertia. When the land is uneven, the height and pitch of the topography shows the potential strength and speed that the energy can move. The greater the peaks and valleys, the more dynamic the forces that can be felt upon the place. Power flows like water. One need only to imagine how water would roll along over a specific landscape to envision how natural energy would move upon it. A place with a lot of steep hills and valleys will have energy that is very intense and restless with potential pockets of stagnation. A place that has rolling hills would have energy like gentle waves upon a lake, which can be soothing.

An area that is largely flat and without obstructions, like a large field or a prairie, can be intense in its own way because energy that has been set into motion can travel very quickly. However, just like water resting on a flat surface, the energy on flat topography will require some sort of directional energy to get it from point A to point B.

If you are looking for a place where the energy is strong yet restful, then it would be recommended to find a building located in mountains. Mountains carry energy that is intense, but also stable, represented by a mountain's rocky features. The rocks, representing the element of earth, would slow down the intense energy. Mountains have an eternal quality about them and are great places to connect with the sacred spirits that watch over the land.

Bodies of Water Both Above and Below Ground

Water is considered to be the blood of our Earth Mother. Earth is a water planet and we are mostly made of water ourselves. The element of water is second only to the element of air in terms of elements needed to sustain life. Water unites all of us. There is an old expression I often share during community gatherings to highlight the unity of water: there are seven seas but only one ocean.

Water carries spiritual energy and is a conduit for electricity, as well as enhancing the intensity of energetic features such as ley lines, vortices, and portals, which I will explain a little further in this chapter in the nonphysical features section. Depending on the health and the flow of water, it can directly impact people and animals that live around it.

Since water is reflective, any water feature will help to enhance what is reflected within it. Whatever is placed within water can be purified, such as when people bathe in a sacred river, and that too can greatly influence a region. Water is like the blood system in our body. And just like us, Earth Mother's blood needs to be kept clean in order to remain healthy. Keeping our waterways clean is like keeping our bodies healthy by only putting good things in them, like nutritious food or clean water. When observing a landscape for good energy, optimal water features would be peacefully flowing over the landscape and reflecting the heavens.

Another way to tell if the water in a landscape you are observing is life inducing and life supporting is to take a closer look at the health of the flora and fauna around it. Not only is it vital for your physical health to know what is happening to the waters around you, it also indicates the spiritual health of a place. *Whatever body of water you are close to must be healthy and alive.* This is obvious for health reasons, but for energetic reasons, any place that is polluted will also affect your emotions and may block energies over time. The more polluted a body of water is, the faster the degradation of your overall well-being, both physically and spiritually.

Waterways will always help to keep things moving. How forceful the movement of water is will determine the way that the energy is delivered to the land surrounding it. In other words, water that is moving gently like a small stream or raging like a river will reflect the energy that you will receive from it.

It is preferable to live in a place where the water is tranquil rather than turbulent. Any place that has a water feature of some kind that flows with clean and healthy water will be conducive to enhancing life. It will be a good place for processing ideas and working in cooperation with others who are of similar mind and philosophy.

Trees, Wildlife, and Other Natural Things

In order to work with the Heart of the Earth technique, it's important to learn about the native plants, trees, and animals of a region so that you can easily understand its health. Energy flows like water, and just like that element, it likes to take the path of least resistance. Its speed and type of energy depends the beings that interact with it, both seen and unseen, as well as the topography and where the Power originated from.

This sacred energy can pool or be pulled in to flow in a certain direction due to the magnetic and electromagnetic forces of the earth. All beings—plants and animals—that come into contact with this sacred current color the energy with their memories and emotions. This includes all of the people and beings who have dwelt upon the land. This influence becomes cumulative and gains force and expression over years and centuries. Take time to get to know your wild neighbors and see how they are faring. Observe their overall health and well-being. This can be the best gauge to see if the land is copacetic for you to live on.

Let us say, for example, that you observe a species of tree that you know, under normal circumstances, should grow to be tall, straight, and strong. However, if you notice that the trees in a specific location seem to be dwarfed or twisted, then it is possible that the energy from that land is hostile, poisoned, or that the soil had been depleted of nutrients over several years.

Observing the species of animals in a region can also give you an idea as to the type of energy that the land holds. Let's pretend that I am in a place where I know there should be many native songbirds. If the place seems quiet because it is missing many of those songbirds, then I can be certain that the land is not conducive to supporting delicate life. This is true regardless of whether the energy that created this was through natural processes or through human carelessness. The opposite can also be true. Imagine that there is an abundance of robust trees, grasses, and other flora even though the soil may not be especially fertile. This is a sign of healthy, nurturing, mother-like energy in the land. The same is true if you find an abundance of wildlife, especially where, under logical circumstances, the numbers should be substantially less.

Pay attention to whether a region is fertile or seems to be an area where decomposition takes place. If you find that the land is barren or stark, this would be a good place to set up a recycling facility or a warehouse that helps things to come to their final destination and speed along decomposition. Building anything that falls in harmony with what the land is doing will always enhance what you are trying to create.

Stones and Other Large Masses of Earth

Stones, boulders, and mountains are like the skeletal system within our own bodies. The element of earth held within stones holds ancient memories. I know this might sound odd, but even in science studying the strata of the earth tells much about the earth's geographical history, in addition to that of past civilizations.

When you say you feel something in your bones, it's the same way stones and crystals can hold memory. Bones retain energy to generate different cells depending on what the body needs: cells to enhance bone density or blood cells to ensure the flow of oxygen and nutrients. Stones and crystals can retain energy like a battery. Earth Mother can activate the stones and crystals within her to generate the energy she needs to remain in harmony. They give physical structure to our planet and, shamanically speaking, hold ancient wisdom and stories that teach us how to live in harmony within ourselves and all of creation.

Crystals versus Stones

Non-precious stones hold different types of information and Power than crystals, semiprecious stones, or precious stones. Common non-precious stones are said to retain the memories of daily life they have witnessed throughout the centuries. Because of this, common stones can be very useful for reflecting upon your life or connecting with the ancient wisdom of the land, often by sitting upon or touching a stone. Different crystals and gems hold energy and memories specific to their type.

For example, the quartz family of crystals are enhancers. They have piezoelectric properties and can easily amplify spiritual energy. In my experience, quartz crystals boost whatever energy runs through them. In the recent past, quartz crystals have been used in the making of watches and communication devices. Other stones, such as hematite, are utilized for grounding and for teaching us how to pace ourselves.

Air Quality

Air is one of the most critical elements to sustain life. It is a dynamic element. The winds of air are like the respiratory system for our Earth Mother. Making sure that you are in a place where the air is clean does more than ensure good physical health. It is a critical component needed to achieve and sustain spiritual health and beneficial Power. This is done by making sure that you do not pollute the air around you with too much noise or light, as well as avoiding doing things that can fill the atmosphere with smog.

Healthy air needs to circulate freely. A place that does not have air moving through it can be stifling and claustrophobic. Air that is stagnant or stuck in a closed system that is not purified can harbor the growth of harmful airborne bacteria that cause infection and disease. The element of air also represents thought and communications. When the air is stuffy, we get sleepy and cannot think clearly. When we are not thinking clearly, miscommunication and accidents happen. Making sure that the air around you is fresh is *key* for a happy place. If the ambience is heavy with energetic or emotional pollution, simple remedies like listening to pleasant music or the soothing sounds of nature can help clear the air.

HUMAN-MADE LAND FEATURES

When assessing the features of the land, we need to consider more than just what we find in the natural world. Just as land affects us, we have also made an impact on land over the centuries. As such, these human impacts must be included when taking an overall look of any place or location. If the land has not been treated properly, there can be very strident energy.

Mining, deforestation, and factories that are reckless in how they treat the environment are classic examples of places that no one wants to be living near. This recklessness is reflected back to us by the pollution causing disease and sickness. However, the opposite is also true. Places where great care has been taken to clean the oceans, plant trees to restore forests, and generally care for the environment will be full of welcoming and flourishing energy.

Buildings

Take a look at the buildings around you. Are the buildings routinely maintained? Is the skyline harsh with the sharp, jagged lines of buildings that compete for space? Or are the buildings inviting and homey, creating a warm community feeling? Sharp edges and points can send energy that cuts like a knife. They cast energy like sharp arrows. A building that has gentle and rounded contours softens the flow of energy so that it is like a friendly current.

Roads

Roads, regardless if they are a goat path or a major highway, transmit energy. As such, they can influence or alter the natural flow of Power of the land. A roadway that is congested and full of hectic, angry people can poison the energy of the land and return it as anxiety and tension to those who live alongside the road.

Roadways that are well managed can still have a lot of people, but will move them along fluidly so that getting to one's destination is smooth and the energy is one of easy, dynamic movement. Living alongside these roads can be very invigorating because the roads act as places where the energy keeps a steady pace and entices people to new adventures.

Roadways that are more like country lanes or small pathways are not only the road "less traveled" physically, but they are paths that carry energy that can feel very private, individual, and more attuned to the natural world. If the roadway or path is too secluded, it can create an energy of stagnation and of being resistant to interaction with the outside world.

Power Lines and Towers

The electromagnetic forces that power lines, tension towers, and telecommunication towers emit are not good at all! They can be harmful and disruptive to the energetics of the natural world. Living close to these structures brings an underlying feeling of being continuously unsettled or scattered. Depending on the intensity of what is being emitted, long-term exposure can create sickness and unease to a point that there are constant disputes or even violence within a home or work place.

Parks

If they are well-kept, parks can be great places of healing and grounding. Parks act as an oasis not only for the natural world, but for us as well because we can connect with the Heart of the land and All Our Relations in a pure way. Parks are places where Sacred Ancestors of the Land and other nature spirits congregate. These locations facilitate growing our connection with nature and deepen loving bonds with each other as friends, family, and community.

Population Density

When it comes to population density, everyone has their own preference. However, the concentration of so much humanity in one space will choke out the natural world, which we need to be healthy. Having a place that is overrun by human structures can create a disassociation with our planet and our wild relatives in nature. Make sure that if you choose to live in a place that is highly populated, such as a city, you have access to nature in some way. Whether it be a park or a healthy plant living within your home, it is vital to *always* have that connection with Earth Mother and the other elements in some way in order to maintain the health of spirit, body, and mind.

Memorials and Graveyards

Memorials carry the echoes of the past and as such they can act as an undercurrent of mood and energy that one may not even be conscious of. How it affects the emotions of a population depends on who or what is being remembered and the manner in which those people or events are being honored. For example, the memorial wall of Vietnam veterans is very beautiful, but if you ever have the chance to visit it in person, the depth of love and sorrow is palpable in the air. As such, the energy in the area around the memorial will be more on the somber side.

Graveyards can be "noisy," like silent cities. Although cemeteries and graveyards might be physically quiet to honor the dead, the spirit activity can truly affect the living. This is because these places are full of all kinds of spirits that congregate, from ghosts to Sacred Ancestors of the Land. Empaths, channels, and mediums will be particularly impacted by graveyards or memorials. Since it may not be easy to avoid these features, just be aware that taking note of the type of energy that a cemetery or memorial carries is similar to paying attention to the type of interaction and energy that you might have within a neighborhood of the living.

Places of Worship

Places of worship are wonderful locations because they welcome and channel divine forces. Depending on the strength of the sacred place, sites of worship can hold within them portals that allow divine energies and sacred beings to interact freely with us and give them easier access to bless our world. The energy and mood of the community surrounding the place of worship will depend on who or what the place of worship is honoring, including the types of beliefs it is reinforcing.

Major Events

Human-made land features and major events leave a social imprint on the land. When researching a location for your home or business, I strongly advise examining the history of the land and of the community. Remember that earth holds memories and echoes can remain that may affect new structures built on the land.

Say, for example, you visit a battlefield. Depending on how violent and brutal the battle was, you will be able to feel the echoes of that historical event. It is not uncommon to have ghosts who are still reenacting what has happened before. The opposite extreme of this type of manifestation is visiting a place where miracles happened or where a great joyous event occurred. A place with positive history will attract benign and life-sustaining beings. The land will also give you feelings of joy, positive energy, and lightness of being when you walk upon it.

The land calls to itself similar types of people that are congruous with its essence. Because of this, similar activities are repeated in a region, consciously or unconsciously, through the centuries. The land will accumulate and grow a particular type of energy exponentially as it acquires and holds on to specific types of memories, feelings, and lessons.

NONPHYSICAL FEATURES OF THE LAND

Just like we have the different systems in our body, our beautiful Earth Mother has similar systems in her own body. She generates her own energetic fields, magnetic and otherwise. You can see it above us whenever there is an electrical storm, or it can be measured scientifically as naturally produced electromagnetic frequencies. These energetic systems can also be felt as sensations in your body as you walk the land itself.

In this section I describe three types of energetic systems that are the most commonly found on the land. It is helpful to be able to identify these if you sense them as you walk the land or an indoor space. These nonphysical features of the land are not related to spirit beings, but make up the natural energetic landscape. It is important to assess if you have any of these energetic features in your space because they can influence the movement and type of energy depending where they are located in your space. If you have ley lines, it's important to know how strong their energetic current is and what type of energy flows within them? If you have a portal, what is being allowed to move in between this physical realm in the energetic realms? If you have a vortex, which direction is Power going in? Is it allowing an influx of spirit energy to bring in more life and vitality, or is it a vortex that is meant for releasing and breaking down that which no longer serves?

Ley Lines

Ley lines are direct streams of energy that can cover many miles, sometimes even whole continents. They help to transmit Earth Mother's energy along the surface to help stimulate communication and the overall rhythm of an area or region. Ley lines are the energetic equivalent of creeks, streams, or great rivers that transport the living energy of our Earth Mother across her surface. The intensity and direction of these ley lines will feel as though you're standing in a moving body of water. The intensity of the sensation depends on the strength of the ley line. Harnessing these lines is a good way to enhance what you are trying to create. Of course, paying attention to the quality of energy that is being carried by the ley lines must also be considered in order to ensure harmony versus unnecessary destruction or chaos.

Ley lines that are strong and directed at a person or location can pull someone under or erode the energy of the land, similar to being pounded upon very strong currents of water. In a further chapter I will explain how to harness the lines in a way that is cooperative and will enrich your life.

These lines of energy crisscross the landscape around the globe and act as the nervous center of our Earth Mother, much like the nervous system that runs throughout your own body. Strong ley lines of energy heighten whatever activity takes place upon the land they run through. It is very much like finding a high voltage wire. If not used correctly, it can blow things apart. However, if harnessed properly, the energy of a ley line can act as a wonderful catalyst, in addition to maintaining what you create. Ley lines will provide a steady stream of energy akin to electricity running through your home or place of work.

Portals

Portals are doorways. They are equivalent to the valves in our circulatory system that ensure blood flows in one direction and does not back up. Portals can be generated by nature or, upon occasion, by humans if there is a tremendous event that happened at a specific location. The energetic frequency the portal is resonating with will determine what type of beings will be attracted to it.

Portals act like doors, swinging one direction or both, depending on their purpose. Portals can allow different spirit beings and energies to come from other dimensions and places into our own if it is a door that swings inward. If a portal is geared to swinging outward, then it is meant to take energy from our world into the spirit and energetic realms. These energetic doorways are channels for universal energy to come to and from our planet connecting us to the whole Universe. Portals that swing in both directions can be harmful. Much like swinging doors in a restaurant, if the waiters do not know which way to go, they can slam into each other. The same can happen with these spiritual doorways. If the portal is opened and not attuned to any particular frequency, it can allow beings that are harmful or chaotic to move in as easily as those who would be beneficial.

Fortunately, it is very unusual to have a portal that would allow random chaotic or demonic spirits into our world. I will describe later in this book how to clean the doorway of a portal and attune it so that only a specific type of being or energy can come through. It is very much like creating a lock and a key and the only ones who have access are the ones with the keys. It is not uncommon for portals to occur naturally and very often they can be felt at sacred sites. At times, portals can be very evident when there is an influx of spirit energy or beings, such as places that are haunted or have been recorded to be visited by divine beings.

Portals are formed when there is a strong convergence of spirit energy and earth energy or when an extremely intense event happens. The opening of the portal is formed at the nexus of the incident. Because of this, portals are very common at sites where there have been wars or great gatherings of impassioned people of a movement or cause. Man-made portals, whether they are made consciously or not, vary in duration as to how long they remain open. Those that occur naturally, because they are part of Earth Mother herself, can endure for many centuries.

The way that you will physically sense a portal is you can feel, or sometimes see from the corner of your eye, energy or spirit beings coming into or out of a place before vanishing. When you are standing in a portal, it is very much like the sensation of being in a physical doorway. You can feel that there is an opening to another place. Portals are not to be feared because they are much like the doors in your home. It is just important to understand what they open into, and how to modulate what comes through and when.

Vortices

Vortices are whirlpools of energy. They act as catalytic forces when moving the energy of our planet. Vortices help to drain and release pressure and toxic energies from the land. They are meant to create functional chaos, which helps to tear down old structures so they can go back into the earth and come back in a new form. Vortices and the areas around them can have a very vertigo-like effect on the human senses. Because of their movement and concentration, vortices can also create a feeling of being in a whirlwind. If you are caught in a strong vortex, it could be very disorienting because you can feel that you are spinning very quickly, like a top. To create stability in an environment, vortices regulate, redirect, and redistribute sacred Power as needed. They ensure that spiritual energy circulates evenly throughout our beautiful planet.

An incoming vortex can help to bring in energy from the spirit realms and will have a very intense, empowering effect. You know that you are in this type of vortex because you might feel a giddy or very dizzying rush of Power that makes you feel stronger, much like having a head rush when you are enjoying a good ride at an amusement park. At the other end of the spectrum, an outgoing vortex can release energy generated by this world and have a draining effect.

If a vortex is born of Earth Mother, it will tend to be bigger and more stable. A vortex that is not natural can be accidentally created by a tremendous amount of chaos coupled with extremely intense emotions that actually create an energetic impression upon a land or building. A vortex, unlike a portal, exists strictly to release the pressure generated by the movement of energy on this side or on the spirit side where the worlds connect. By its very nature, a vortex will appear or disappear wherever or whenever our precious Earth Mother needs to equalize energy. From a shaman's perspective, the creation of a vortex is similar to a lightning strike.

⁓ EXERCISE ⁓
USING A PENDULUM TO DETERMINE AN ENERGETIC LAND FEATURE

In addition to physical sensations, you can detect an energetic feature by using a pendulum. The pendulum you use does not need to be anything fancy, it just needs to have enough weight to be able to swing back and forth at the end of a string or chain.

To begin, simply hold the string or chain between your index finger and thumb with at least three to four inches between your hand and the weight at the bottom. Walk to where you suspect or sense there is an energetic feature. If it is a ley line, the pendulum will swing back and forth in a straight line. If the pendulum swings more strongly in one direction than another, it is showing you the direction of the flow of the land's energy.

If the pendulum moves in a cross or square formation, then you have found a portal. When this happens, stop the pendulum from moving and ask the pendulum which direction the portal opens. Then begin swinging the pendulum again. If it moves in a clockwise manner, it means the portal opens into our world. If it moves in a counterclockwise fashion, then the portal goes into the spirit world. If the pendulum only moves in the square or the cross pattern, then you have an energetic doorway that swings both ways.

If your pendulum moves in a circle, it has located a vortex. Just like when the pendulum finds a portal, its movement clockwise or counterclockwise indicates that the vortex is bringing power into this dimension or releasing energy into the spirit world respectively. The movement and intensity of the pendulum will mimic the movement and intensity of the Power flowing through the land.

A pendulum can also be used to detect the direction of the flow of sacred Power. As you hold the pendulum, ask for the pendulum to begin to swing in the direction where the energy flow is coming from. Turn to squarely face the direction that was indicated. Then ask the pendulum if you are correctly facing into the flow of energy. If the pendulum moves forward and back like someone who is nodding their head and saying yes, then you are facing in the proper direction.

If the pendulum swings from side to side as if someone is shaking their head and saying no, then continue to slowly turn toward the direction that the pendulum is indicating until it becomes the yes movement. If you want to know how strong the flow of energy is, face the direction in which the energy is flowing from and ask the pendulum to mimic the intensity of the flow. When you are facing the proper direction, the pendulum should swing forward and back in front of you doing the yes motion. A gentle movement indicates a smaller or weaker source of Power. A greater movement shows a bigger or more forceful current. The way that you can determine the perimeter of an energetic phenomena is by seeing where the pendulum swings the strongest. This is the epicenter of the energetic feature. Walk outward from the center until the pendulum drastically slows down or stops moving. This will show you the edge of the ley line, portal, or vortex.

Of course, there are variations and combinations of the features that I have mentioned above, but for now this will suffice. The strength of any of these energetic features will determine how much they can affect you. If they are very powerful, then it will be a matter of learning how to live with these influences in your life. If the feature in question is weaker or more receptive to being influenced because the energy from it is clean and neutral, then it will be possible to interact with these energetic features. When you're able to interact with these energetic features, you will be able to use them to enhance what you want to develop on your property, create stronger protections, and enrich life in all areas.

Spirit Beings and Other Unseen Residents

It is extremely common to have other beings take up residence on the land who had been there long before you. I'm not talking about the animals, plants, or trees. I'm talking about spiritual beings. Spirit beings can be attached to a location because they are a part of the land, because of unfinished business, or because your activities have attracted them. What I typically find is many people are afraid of these beings and feel that unseen neighbors should be exorcised. This is unnecessary and as you will find out, this reaction is usually undesirable because of the problems it can cause. Just like you have physical neighbors who mean you no harm and can coexist peacefully with them, so it is with these unseen beings.

Much like living and being in a good community, making friends with the spirits and beings of nature is just a good policy. Spirit beings can help to bring you protection and can bring timely messages and healing energy, if you befriend them. The same rules to developing a good relationship with a human being apply to growing a good relationship with your unseen neighbors. It's similar to inviting a well-known friend over in order to make them feel welcome. Sticking to clear guidelines of interaction, having mutual respect, and good house rules ensure a stable and healthy relationship that can grow into a strong friendship as the years go by. Let's go over just a few types of spirit beings that would be relevant for you to know when you follow this practice of the Heart of the Earth.

Sacred Ancestors of the Land: These are *extremely* powerful and ancient entities. Everyone has experienced these beings, although they may not have been aware of who they were interacting with. If you have gone to a place in nature and felt a very kind and wise presence smiling and welcoming you, then you've experienced the Sacred Ancestors of the Land. Sometimes they send dreams and will also send messages through animals and other signs to interact with human beings. They are the guardians of the land. The Sacred Ancestors of the Land are extremely benign and incredibly patient.

If you welcome the Sacred Ancestors of the Land, they will feel like a warm and compassionate grandmother or grandfather energy. Having them upon your land is a great honor and blessing! When they appear, the Sacred Ancestors of the Land will usually take on the form of an elder. It is always proper to welcome them with great respect. Speaking to them and sharing your stories is a way of honoring them. You may find that you can feel their energy is strongest at a certain place. Typically, you can find them around trees, large bodies of water, or big tracts of land, such as mountains. As gentle as Sacred Ancestors of the Land are, if you anger one, great misfortune can happen, including the destruction of buildings and whole regions. However, befriending Sacred Ancestors of the Land brings tremendous blessings to all who work or live where the Ancestors reside.

Nature Spirits: Nature spirits are entities that are the children of the land. They are known throughout many cultures and have several names, such as the menehune of Hawaii, the dwarfs of Europe, and the jogah of the Iroquois. Don't be fooled, nature spirits may be small, but they are mighty and many! They travel between what we experience as three-dimensional reality Earth and the spiritual manifestation of Earth. They are very wise, but can be very capricious. They are fiercely protective of those they are fond of and just as quick to punish those whom they are not fond of.

At times, nature spirits can be seen as points of light or shadows darting quickly. To befriend them is to have a strong ally. Not all places have nature spirits. You will know if a place does because you will feel a presence of curiosity about you. Nature spirits' way of being is very quick-witted and very friendly, if they desire to interact with you. It should be noted that nature spirits are *not* poltergeists. However, it is not uncommon with nature spirits to have objects disappear and reappear throughout your home.

Nature spirits will feel very much like small guests observing what is going on throughout your home and will give feedback on what they see. They understand the idea of rules and structure, so a set of house rules that everyone agrees to is a good way to be comfortable with them. They appreciate gifts, such as small tokens of beauty, and acts of kindness to nature, such as feeding birds.

Sacred Ancestors: Sacred Ancestors are the spirits of those people whom we love who have crossed over and have completed their spiritual journey. They choose to be with us and are not lost souls. Some Sacred Ancestors come to protect, some to advise, and some to give strength and comfort to those they knew in life.

Honoring and asking for help of the Sacred Ancestors will help to bring a warmth and protection to your home that is not easily rivaled. This depends, of course, on the individual who chooses to return and what you ask for them to assist you with. For example, say that you had a loving grandmother who watched over you in life and was always very good at healing. As a Sacred Ancestor, she could help give protection against and speed up recovery from illness.

Ghosts: I mention this type of entity not because they are desirable, but because it is not unusual to stumble across one. There are two types of ghosts. The first type is that of a person or an animal that has died but has not completed their sacred journey to become a purified soul. These kinds of beings are harmful, but not because they intend to be. It is because the energetic frequency of the dead is very different than that of the living. If they are around the living for too long, the conflicting energies of life and death can create misfortune, illness, and increase arguments within a home or work place.

The remedy here is to compassionately ask for that soul to continue their journey back to the Great Spirit. You can also ask sacred beings, such as a Sacred Ancestor or other divine being, to assist by guiding the earthbound soul to where it needs to go. If you find that the ghost is still haunting your place in a way that is frightful or toxic, do not engage! It is best to call someone who is trained in these matters escort this resistant soul from this earth realm to where they need to be.

The second type of ghost is not sentient; instead, it's a part of a land's memory and is stuck reenacting an event. As mentioned previously, the land retains memories. If an event is traumatic or euphoric enough, its imprint can remain on the land and keep on repeating, much like replaying a video that you are streaming.

Malevolent Beings: This type of spirit being consciously chooses to be harmful or evil. Malevolent beings thrive on all things toxic and feed on pain and suffering. I am very pleased to say that malevolent beings are not very prevalent. I recommend *not* engaging with these beings at all and seeking expert help immediately! Trying to do it yourself is simply asking for trouble. There are people who are trained to discern what specific type of malevolent being is afflicting a location and know how to take the proper steps to keep everyone safe while extracting the entity.

INDOOR FEATURES

Assessing the lay of the land inside a building is equally as important as paying attention to the outside topography. Several things can affect the flow of Power in regard to a building. The distribution of rooms and their shape can affect the intensity of the flow, as well as its direction.

For example, some older homes have rooms that are circular, semicircular, hexagonal, or semihexagonal. These shapes have a tendency to create a vortex of energy and will have a penchant to hold on to emotional and energetic impressions more than other types of room shapes. These room shapes will hold on to the echo of events that have happened in the past. In my experience, rooms of circular or hexagonal shape seem to have a feeling of being lost in time. It is not unusual for ghosts, if they are around, to linger in this type of room and peer outside of a window. It does not make these room shapes undesirable, just be mindful of their tendencies.

Another thing to consider is the people who have lived or worked in a space in the past. Each time the resident of a home or work space changes, they leave behind an energetic residue and impressions of daily events. When you move into a space, you might find yourself acting in ways similar to an archaeologist or geologist, reading what has happened during a particular era in your space, perhaps finding similar historic patterns. As mentioned before, the land sends out its own unique energy signature and subconsciously, we respond to it. It is not uncommon to have a similar type of community, family, or individual coming to a place over and over again. Similar events will keep on repeating if they are harmonic to the land, but with different "characters" reenacting the scene.

The style of dwelling must also be factored in when considering its impact on the natural flow of Power and how it expresses itself in physical form. For example, a single level dwelling, such as a ranch style house, would have a quicker and more natural flow of Power in relation to the land compared to a dwelling with multiple floors, such as an apartment building or dorm. These factors also apply to office buildings. The more people, rooms, and floors in a building actually magnifies the original expression of the land or a significant event that happened upon it.

An additional consideration is to take into account the placement and intended use of a room and making sure those are in harmony with the direction or Arrow that would support it. This idea will be detailed in chapter 6.

THE ROLE OF EACH ROOM

Now, I would like to talk about the role of each type of room that can be found in a home, dorm, work place, etc. For those of you who live in studio apartments or other single room spaces, your space can be broken down into areas or sections that act like rooms. You will use the same methods and techniques, but you would be applying them as if each area were a room of its own.

Hallways, Corridors, and Stairwells

Corridors of any type act as channels for Power to flow through, connecting different rooms to each other. Since hallways act as channels and connections, they behave like the element of spirit. This is why it is important to never let a hallway become cluttered. In Native American spiritual traditions, all things are practical and spiritual. Therefore, in addition to the spiritual need for a lack of clutter, the practical standpoint is that a hallway should never be cluttered for the sake of safety.

From a spiritual point of view, clutter prevents the Breath of the Great Spirit from moving freely and giving life and health to all who are in a dwelling. Choking a hallway with bric-a-brac would be akin to someone constricting your throat. Ultimately, your dwelling would not be able to "breathe" and would become a very unpleasant place to maneuver. The same guidelines apply to stairwells, for they have the same function as a hallway, except that they move the sacred energy vertically to connect the Power between floors.

Storage Spaces

Storage spaces, such as closets, attics, or crawl spaces, retain the memory of a place. Depending on what these storage spaces are filled with, they can either store or drain energies. These areas are aligned with the element of earth. You should always store items that actively enrich your life, not a hodgepodge of useless or forgotten possessions.

Have you ever had an area in your dwelling that is full of stuff that you don't want to deal with and you hide it away? Of course, you always swear that you will get around to it…but that moment never comes around. Ultimately, when you do have to revisit this area, it becomes a much greater project than if you handled it all along. From a practical standpoint, this is self-evident. From a spiritual standpoint, this clutter could keep you locked into old patterns and hold you back from evolving. Having a storage area that is just holding clutter is very much like someone who is lost in the past, not paying attention to the present and paying even less attention to the future. From a safety standpoint, clutter is a health and fire hazard.

Bathrooms

The bathroom should be a place of release and recovery, with the element of water strongly represented. I know this sounds funny. The idea of releasing, of course, is represented when you are relieving yourself. But, it's also represented when you are taking a bath or shower to wash away all of the tensions of the day—physical, mental, and spiritual tensions. Once you have completed taking care of yourself, you feel refreshed. The bathroom is also a place of privacy.

From a practical standpoint, it is important to keep the bathroom clean, which is obvious for hygienic reasons. From a spiritual standpoint, it is important to keep the bathroom clean to make sure that all unwanted energetic residues clinging to your spirit are washed away. Sometimes the toxins that your body and soul get rid of can be seen as the rings that form in the sink, tub, or toilet. When the bathroom smells clean, it is a welcoming place to do whatever restoring or releasing is necessary to feel good about yourself and get on with the day. A bathroom does not have to be fancy to fulfill its purpose. Only place items in the bathroom that are needed to feel safe and private so that you can present yourself the way that you wish to the world.

Kitchen

The kitchen is one of the areas in which all the elements must be present in order for it to fulfill its function. The element of fire is present through your source of heat for cooking. It doesn't matter if the source is electric- or gas-based. Electricity is considered to be liquid fire and as you recall, fire is symbolic of the Breath of the Creator as a transformative element. Fire helps transform whatever ingredients you may place into a pot or pan and converts them from simple ingredients into a delicious dish. The element of fire brings warmth by heating your food and drinks, which can be especially pleasurable on a cold day. The kitchen is where meals are prepared that are savored and enjoyed by us and those we love, especially during holiday seasons.

The element of water is represented by the sink and appliances we use to wash our dishes and utensils. Just like in the bathroom, this element helps to restore and refresh us. Hygiene is also important in the kitchen, both from the practicality of being sanitary and from the spiritual standpoint of it being aesthetically pleasing. The element of water helps restore dirty dishes into clean ones. Water also washes raw ingredients so they can be ready to be prepared into a meal. When water is added to a recipe, ingredients are transformed and are turned to something new, such as coffee or soup. In the kitchen, water also represents health, as it's often the room we go to for drinking water.

The element of air is represented in the kitchen by the way that our appliances are vented, in addition to any windows. Air deals with communication, how we think of life, and mental health. The aromas in the air that may come from a kitchen can either invite us in or turn our stomachs. There are times when we accidentally burn things and the smell of smoke reminds us to focus. Having a kitchen area that is vented is critical for the sake of safety and so that the air does not become rancid. Paying attention to smells that are pleasant welcomes us into the kitchen. Making sure that there is plenty of air and air circulation is another way to guarantee that the energy in the kitchen is as it should be.

The element of earth is represented by the counters, utensils, plates, or other appliances that do not deal directly with cooking or washing. This element is all about manifestation and building. Earth holds memory. This is represented by the food you make that you put in your body to help build your cells, which will remain with you for the next several years. Earth likes routine and structure, represented by mealtimes and other habits, such as cleaning out the refrigerator. I know at times it can be difficult and "biology experiments" can grow in the refrigerator or freezer from time to time. However, creating routines of what to rotate or what to throw out is a good habit to have and ensures that your provisions are fresh. Keep your work areas clean and tidy.

The element of spirit is found in the overall feeling of the kitchen, similar to how the Great Spirit is everywhere but not necessarily seen. What type of feeling does your kitchen have? Does it feel like a place of drudgery or is it a cozy nook you can go to enjoy something that will refresh you for the day? What you use for decorating the kitchen should uplift your spirits and be relatively easy to maintain. Again, it does not have to be glamorous or luxurious, but clean, simple, and inviting.

The kitchen is a place of nourishment and reflects a person's self-worth. What you feed yourself with and how you do it reflects how you value yourself and others. This is not meant to be a statement of judgment. It doesn't mean that you need to have gourmet, expensive foods to show that you care for yourself or others.

Rather, it is making sure that what you place in the kitchen takes the form of basic nourishing foods, such as natural foods instead of highly processed foods. Don't get me wrong, I enjoy fun foods myself. My personal favorite is chocolate. I joke that I worship the goddess "Chocolatina" a little bit every day. However, it's important that the majority of foods you purchase are healthy and nourishing. It does not matter whether you cook or not, it's just about taking the time to make the best choices to honor your body.

It is said that you are what you eat because what you eat and drink provides the resources for your body to build on. Food acts as Medicine because the nutrition you take in bolsters your immune system. Take care that you have what your body really needs readily available and that your kitchen provides you with the proper way to prepare it. The kitchen is the cornerstone of your home where you prepare this Medicine for you and others.

Bedrooms

The bedroom should be a place of rest and recovery. It should be one of the places in your home where you can safely be yourself and be rejuvenated. The dominant element here is that of fire. I know at first glance this may seem counterintuitive. Remember that this divine element represents the life force. Every day you need to make time to restore yourself.

It is also the place where there can be romantic fire, a place that encourages a deeper connection between loving couples and the celebration of their chemistry. Fire definitely needs to be represented, regardless of what other elements are dominant in the bedroom.

This is a room that should be private and hold things that are near and dear to your heart. Even within a shared bedroom, there should be spaces within the room that are unique to each of the individuals that sleep there, whether it be a dorm mate, sibling, or a life partner.

Study/Library

A study or library should be a place of learning and intellectual stimulation. Not surprisingly, this room is represented by air, the element of thought. This is the room that encourages constructive daydreams and the development of thoughts or plans for the future.

Even if you do not have a room that can act as a formal study or library, it is a good idea to always have a nook or corner in your home dedicated to this. Filling this space with personal things that inspire you will assist you in expanding your vision of yourself and the world. This room should not be like the sleepy libraries that you see in the movies. Yes, enjoy having different reading material for entertainment, but remember this is the place where you store food for thought. Make sure that what is stored here is a mixture of useful information, in addition to being pleasurable.

Garage

As I mentioned before, places of storage represent the element of earth. However, because a garage also stores forms of transportation, the element of water will also be present.

The garage should always be a place of movement. Make sure that all items such as tools or seasonal items are stored in a way that is easy to access. Otherwise, you will find this becomes a place of major clutter where in the end not even your car, motorcycle, or bikes and wagons will have a place to be put away.

The garage is representative of our desire to create and to explore. Many people use a garage as a place to have a workbench or workshop. Make sure that you have everything you need to make it a safe place as well, since many people store hazardous materials, such as fuels, paints, and gardening chemicals.

SANCTUARY SPACE

For your own sake and overall well-being, you must create a sanctuary space, even if it's just a tiny portion of a room. All elements should be present in this space, with your own personal element being dominant! The mood and energy of this room should help you feel your best so you can recover from a bad day or add an extra boost to your morale if you're having a good one.

These sanctuary spaces should have the ability to calm you down, recenter yourself, and revitalize you.

For each one of us, a sanctuary space is different. For some people, their sanctuary needs to be a place of perfect quiet. For others, such as myself, it is a place filled with activities, but sprinkled with options of rest. The idea of a sanctuary space is one where you can get away from the world. It is a primal need that we never really outgrow. At some point in our childhoods, we all had our little hideaway spots. A sanctuary space should be a private place that celebrates your own unique spirit. Let me describe three basic forms of a sanctuary space.

Workshop or Studio

A creative space is one that is usually filled with options of different activities such as painting, woodworking, jewelry making, or machining. The idea of a space like this is to give you an outlet to express yourself. This is ideal for people who find making things to be very therapeutic. This type of sanctuary would be considered to be most aligned with the energy of the southeast point of the Medicine Wheel.

As fun and exciting as a creative space might be, it could all too easily melt into a huge mass of disorganized chaos if not properly maintained. Take time to figure out where you are going to store tools, materials, and reference books (if you use them). Make a routine. Figure out how much time you need to set up for whatever activity you are going to do and make sure to *budget twice as much time for cleaning up afterwards.* Yes, I know this practice will shorten your time for creativity, but you will become grateful for this good habit as you become accustomed this routine.

The reason I recommend that your cleaning up time be twice as long as set up time is because this allows for you not only to wash and store your materials and tools where they belong, but allows for you to reacclimate and avoid the "culture shock" of moving from a space of personal creativity to a space of regular responsibilities.

Meditation Room

There are those of us who prefer to be at rest and at complete peace versus being busy. A meditation room is for exactly that. Whatever is placed in a meditation space should make you relaxed and help you unwind. The time spent in a meditation space is insulated from the hustle and bustle of the rest of your household. Place items, decorations, and pictures that allow you to move beyond your mind chatter and troubles so you can deeply relax. I recommend having an array of comfortable pillows, blankets, or bolsters so that you may sit or lie down in comfort.

Although a meditation space may not have as much of an inclination to go into cluttered chaos as a creative space, it might have the tendency to become stagnant and stale. Make sure to keep this area current and introduce fresh energy as needed. Take care to give yourself enough time to transition from your state of deep relaxation before going back to your daily tasks. I still insist on keeping the rule of thumb of giving twice as much time to come back into everyday life as you take to get into your relaxed state. This is because the transition from peace to everyday noise can feel extremely harsh, especially if you are an empath.

Den/Family Room/Recreation Room

There are some people who prefer to share their sanctuary space with their loved ones. These are spaces that are meant for families and friends to be able to recharge by being in each other's company. Since these types of rooms could lend themselves to too much activity and noise, I suggest arranging the room so that the environment can turn from that of a joyful gathering or party into one of a soothing and relaxing evening. There should be plenty of comfortable places to sit and flat surfaces to set refreshments upon.

The definition of a soothing time is different for each of us. If you enjoy watching movies, shows, or sports, make sure that you have the technology to accommodate that, but balance that time with turning electronics off so there can be meaningful conversations and personal quality time with those you love. Remember that these are places that represent you as a group and as a family. Whatever is placed here should be whatever collectively gives you solace.

PART 2
Evaluate, Plan, and Create Your Space

Five

EVALUATING YOUR SPACE AND ITS COMPATIBILITY

NOW THAT WE HAVE covered all of the basic concepts and exercises, you are ready to begin evaluating your space. The following chapters will give you the necessary information to see what you are working with in order to build your space in harmony with your own desires, as well as those of the land you are on.

As you embark on creating your space, you will need a notepad, pen, and a good compass. It is vital that you take concise and detailed notes as you assess your surroundings. Being organized will make it much easier for you to know where to apply which technique as we go further along in this book. Admittedly, some of the initial steps may be tedious, but you will only need to do them once. The rest of the steps will be much more enjoyable because you will be able to use your creativity and focus on catering to your own tastes.

STEP ONE: DEFINING YOUR WANTS AND NEEDS

Whether determining if a place is worth acquiring or updating your current space, give yourself ample time to make a list of both your requirements (your absolute must-haves that are nonnegotiable, such as having ample sunlight if you like bright settings) and your wishes (what would be nice to have but you are willing to be flexible about, such as how many windows a room has). Remember, the idea is to set things up so that you can be comfortable in that place for a long time. Therefore, take a long-term approach to the goals for your home or work space and what you want the space to do for you. Here are some things to consider:

- Make sure you identify the difference between absolute necessities and desires that you are willing to be flexible about.
- Include a list of what costs, both financially and energetically, you are willing to pay to be at the location.
- How do you want your space to nurture you and your loved ones? What do you absolutely need in order to feel safe and secure in that place?
- What type of community do you prefer to be in or have easy access to?
- Define what makes a home or work space perfect for your purposes.

Obviously, no place will ever be 100 percent perfect, but being able to articulate what it is that you need will make it much easier in determining if a place is worth putting effort into. If you are looking to acquire a new piece of real estate, this will be tremendously helpful to your agent in being able to find a property that is the closest match to your requirements.

STEP TWO: A SHORTCUT TO DETERMINE IF A PLACE IS WORTH A SECOND LOOK

In order to avoid having to do detailed work for every space you encounter, let me give you a shortcut. In addition to the considerations mentioned in step one, I will give you one more step to make it easy to determine if a place deserves a second look.

For this extra step, take accurate compass readings of both the front and back entrances (we will look at compass readings more in-depth shortly with the exercise on page 107) and record the direction of each. The direction of the front entrance attracts the type of energy and opportunities the location will call to itself. The rear entrance defines the challenges and overall rewards that will be accomplished. If these compass points are not in alignment with the type of manifestations that you wish to bring into your life, it is better to continue looking elsewhere.

If you choose to pursue a building that is not in alignment with what you are trying to create and how you wish to live, you may find yourself in a constant battle with hardships. You might also be left with a persistent sense of unease that escalates to low-level anxiety, which can ruin your health over time.

On the other hand, if you find that the compass points of the front and rear entrances are in alignment with your life's intentions, then put that place on your list of potential dwellings to investigate further. Occupying a place that agrees with what you are trying to accomplish will supply you with abundance in all ways for many years to come.

Flow of a Building's Energy Is Reversed

Paying attention to the flow of energy in a dwelling is paramount. It is very rare, but upon occasion you'll have a house or building where the energy flow is reversed, meaning that the energy flows from the rear entrance to the front entrance. If you would like to confirm the flow of energy through a building, use the pendulum exercise on page 83. Sometimes simple observation is all that is necessary.

You may have noticed that there are dwellings where people tend to use the back door instead of the front door constantly. This is a very good indicator that the flow of energy is reversed throughout the building. It is not possible nor recommended to attempt to correct the flow of energy. It would be akin to the antiquated practice of "correcting" a person for being left-handed and forcing them to write with their right hand. If you tried such a foolish experiment on a dwelling, all you would accomplish is bringing in unending rampant chaos, and the dwelling would act as if it were constantly going into sheer madness. Remember that using these techniques means working in cooperation with the land, *not* against it!

A dwelling with a reversed energy flow will have you look at your obstacles, or areas you need to become stronger in, first. The building will also give you glimpses of the end result of what your efforts will produce first before the resources to make it manifest come to you. Although initially it might feel a little topsy-turvy, it does not mean that it is a bad place to be in. Consider this dwelling to be like a trusted friend who is a problem-solver and able to foresee how things will potentially end before an undertaking is started. Like this trusted friend, this dwelling will be able to anticipate and resolve issues before they happen. The reversed energy in this dwelling will also help you strategize on how best to use future resources that will be coming so that everything else can be easier before taking action.

☙ EXERCISE ❧
GETTING A PROPER COMPASS READING

In order to be able to get proper orientation of your location or potential dwelling, you will need a compass. It is okay to use an electronic compass on a smartphone app, but in my opinion it is much better to use a high quality physical compass. I personally use a Silva Guide Model 426, which can be used for orienteering. Remember that all compasses can be influenced and have less accuracy depending on what is in their environment. If you're using an electronic compass, fluctuations can occur depending on the strength of the signal that it is receiving from the internet or satellites. If using a compass with a physical arrow that depends on magnetism, you have to be aware of the amount of metal that exists in your surroundings. This includes things like key chains or flashlights.

When you read from a compass, you must take a reading more than once and write it down each time. I personally recommend taking about three or four readings. Write down what you get each time and then take the average.

Basic Compass Reading

One of the most basic things to know about compass reading is that one end of the needle always points north. On mountaineering/orienteering compasses, it is almost always the red end that points north, but it is a good idea to test your compass before starting to use it. If you are north of the equator in North America, Europe, or Asia, stand facing the sun around noon with your compass resting in your hand in front of you. Whichever end of the needle points toward the sun is south and the end that points at you is north. If you are south of the equator, the north end points toward the sun and the south end points at you.

To read your compass, hold it steadily in your hand so the baseplate is level and the direction-of-travel arrow (printed on the baseplate) is pointing straight away from you. Hold the compass about halfway between your face and waist in a comfortable arm position with your elbow bent and compass held close to your stomach. Look down at the compass and see where the needle points.

Turn the compass dial (the housing) until the north mark and the direction-of-travel arrow are lined up with the north end of the needle. Since the direction-of-travel arrow is usually two parallel lines on the base of the compass housing, a common saying to memorize this is "red in the shed." Once the red arrow is lined up with the direction-of-travel arrow, you will know where north is. Note the direction or the degrees, if your compass has them.

When getting the bearings of the front and back entrances of a dwelling, make sure that you have your back to the building. If you live in an apartment, the orientation will be from your own front door. If you do not have a balcony or back door the compass point for back of the apartment would be exactly 180 degrees from the front door. In other words, if your apartment or work space does not have a back entrance but your front entrance faces east, then the "rear entrance" would be west. For shorthand, use an arrow symbol to indicate the front entrance.

Figure 4: Front Entrance Symbol

For the back entrance, use a symbol of the fletching of the arrow. If you are in a place that has more than one front or back entrance, then use the bearings of the main front door and the main back door.

Figure 5: Back Entrance Symbol

In step three, we'll use these readings to asses the energetic features of a dwelling. Please also refer to the reference list of energetic properties in the appendix.

Step Three: Assessing Features of Your Place

As stated previously, each compass point has unique benefits and challenges and is watched over by a specific sacred Arrow. Because of this, it is necessary to see which way a dwelling is oriented to help determine if it is worth considering.

In addition to factoring in the spiritual influences in relation to which direction you are facing, the orientation of a building will also determine how much sunlight and moonlight you will get every day. Do not overlook this critical detail because sunlight and moonlight will influence your daily moods and how content you will feel in your home or work space. Over time, this will have a direct and profound impact on your overall mental health and well-being. I am a person who feels the best during the daytime and needs lots of sunlight. Conversely, I have a friend who is more of a night owl and prefers soft or indirect light. As such, I have chosen a place where my work space and a balcony face south. My friend has chosen a home where her relaxation space faces north and her home office faces west. Let's look at what a house attracts depending on what direction it's facing.

Eastern Facing

The east is the place where the sun rises. It brings the Breath of the Great Spirit, the dawning of a new day, and fresh beginnings. Any space that faces this direction will always attract what is new. East helps to highlight original ideas, rejuvenates structures, and introduces brand new routines. The east is the perfect orientation for starting new stages of life such as a marriage, raising a family, and any businesses that deal with renovations, innovations, or law and order.

Southern Facing

A space that faces south will be full of wisdom, folly, and energy of youth. It is the direction of bold experimentation and the willingness to go joyfully into unexplored territory. There will always be something going on in a southern space and it is a place that will draw many people. This will always be a location that is full of activity and promotes networking. A house with a front entrance facing south is perfect for starting the second stage of your life, developing your creativity, or starting your life over.

Businesses that thrive facing this direction are those that deal with agriculture, retail, advertising, hospitality, the humanities, and mental healing. The challenge of a space that faces south is that it would be a place in perpetual motion if it wasn't balanced. A southern space can be very inconsistent in its pacing and rhythms.

Western Facing

The west is the place where the sun sets. It is where you see the velvety dark blue of the night sky filled with stars. It is a time of rest and peaceful introspection. If your space faces west, then it is a space that will prefer to be quiet. A home that faces this direction will be a place that carefully selects and gathers who and what it attracts to itself. It is a place that will facilitate building a solid reputation and become well-established.

A western facing space is perfect if you want to bring more stability into your life and wish to find your true self. It is a place of stillness. The challenge of a western space is that it can be given to extremes. On one hand, it could be so still that it becomes stagnant. On the other hand, the space could be full of profound emotions that hang on to energy, producing low level anxiety or restlessness.

The perfect businesses to face west are those that rely on building a reputation and having a high profile. That might include event planners, government offices, or those in the media. This is an excellent direction for an inventor, those trying to manifest what they feel and see, and those who are involved in engineering, computers, and technology. A western place bestows endurance and will attract others who are kindred spirits. West is an ideal direction for networking.

Northern Facing

A space that faces to the north is one that will be stable. It is a place of wisdom and of handicrafts. Spaces that are oriented north are best suited for those who are in a stage of letting go or are in need of profound healing. Homes or businesses that are oriented to the north are ideal for those who like to work with their hands.

Businesses that prosper oriented north include those that deal with investments, real estate, fabrications, trades, and mortuary sciences, or those in the medical or veterinary fields. The direction of north supports healing of the body and the environment. Northern sites are ideal for those who are holistic practitioners or wish to grow more profoundly into their spirituality.

The challenge of the direction of north is getting stuck in old ways of being because this direction tends to focus on stability and building solid foundations. If you are not careful, you can become stuck and lost in time in a northern facing space. North can bring the challenge of accepting what is new because there is a reliance on what has *always* worked. There is the danger of narrow-mindedness and the inability to accept change.

Locations Facing the Walking Winds

We go now from the cardinal points, which are stable, anchoring energies, to describing spaces that face the between points, which are also known as the Walking Winds. Any spaces that face the points between will always be places of constant but fluid movement.

Northeast Facing

Spaces that face northeast might leave you feeling like you're living in limbo. The northeast is known as the Place of Becoming. This is the compass point of infinite potential, but no clear or specific path. Locations that face this direction will always be in a state of flux, so they require constant dedication to purpose to stay the course. Northeast spaces are wonderful for finally shedding the remnants of an old skin and looking into the future with a clean slate. A space oriented northeast is meant to be a haven of safe experimentation. It's a space that can also help with getting one's bearings when feeling disoriented after leaving behind an old life, not yet comfortable in the new one. This is the compass point that can reset a person, project, or situation into a fresh and more vibrant way of life.

Businesses that do well in northeast spaces include those dealing with grief, trauma, or addiction counseling, auction houses; and executive and consultative services. A challenge of this direction can include leaving you feeling as if you do not belong to any place or very lonely. A building oriented northeast will have a tendency to attract energy of procrastination, idle daydreaming, and distraction if you lose your focus or motivation.

Southeast Facing

Spaces that face the southeast are places that support building community and the development of families and groups. When a place faces southeast, it will help build one's identity. Southeast spaces are perfect if you are starting over or recovering from a traumatic event. Locations facing this direction are superb for the gathering and growing of communities and expanding networks. A southeast space will attract people who are willing to devote and dedicate themselves to causes that are larger than themselves.

Businesses that do well in southeast spaces include organizations that help others, spiritual centers, cosmetology businesses, or construction and contracting. The challenge of southeast is that because it is a space of rapid growth, things can quickly get out of control by becoming too scattered or unwieldy. It can become a site that draws too many strong personalities where *everyone* wants to be chief and no one wants to be part of the tribe.

Southwest Facing

Places that face the southwest are places of tremendous power! Southwest spaces attract wealth and fame. These are places for those who wish to rise and be recognized. The energy in southwest locations commands your total focus and unswerving devotion to your goals. Depending on how dedicated you are, Earth Mother will respond in kind to provide you with the people and resources you need to concretely build and reach your goals.

Businesses that do well in southwest spaces include those that deal with commodities, investments, banking; and the healing of animals and nature; design of any type; and science, especially development and research. The challenges of southwest energy can include becoming consumed by work or greed, or developing a zealous fixation that can recklessly throw the rest of your life out of balance. It will be crucial to constantly keep in mind and religiously practice balancing the needs of the self versus the needs of others. It will also be important to nurture yourself outside of work and spend quality time with your close relationships.

Since the southwest holds the power of the thunderstorm, it holds a catalytic energy to move things very quickly. However, if the energy of the southwest is not handled carefully, it can blow apart in a fast and spectacular fashion.

Northwest Facing

The northwest is the direction where the moon's influence rides high. Spaces oriented to the northwest assist with releasing an old life and creating space to safely plan the new one that comes after it. Spaces that face the northwest are the perfect places to start shedding an old skin and begin deep healing. These are ideal locations for privacy and developing deep relationships that can last a lifetime. Northwest energy encourages you to give yourself permission to be your authentic self without fear or reservation. The gift of a space that faces northwest is that it will teach you the balance of giving and receiving. It creates an environment that shows you how to be healthy and when to be vulnerable. Spaces that face this direction require you to ask what you need and allow yourself to receive it.

Businesses that fare the best facing northwest are places of therapy and rehabilitation. This includes lines of work related to corrections and places that improve one's health through quitting bad habits and embracing healthier ones. The northwest is also a good energy to help guide those who need to heal from life transitions and guide others to get their bearings after unexpected major changes. Other businesses that do well in northwest space include those dealing with travel, advising, academia, and the culinary arts.

The challenge of a dwelling that faces northwest can be remaining stuck in one's uncertainty or fear of letting go of the old. The energy of the northwest can also make it hard to release bad patterns of giving too much and losing oneself in the service of others.

Understand and Interpret How Sacred Power Moves through the Landscape

The front of a space, house, or building can be considered to be its mouth. The direction the front is facing will determine the energy that most easily flows into it. The rear of your space, home, or building would be considered its seat. The direction that the seat is facing defines how the resulting energy will manifest once the energy flowing through the dwelling is used. This manifested energy becomes the momentum to start the cycle over again, completing the Sacred Hoop.

Say, for example, you have a space with a front that faces east. As stated in the previous section, this would be a place that attracts new beginnings and ideas, vibrant energy, and the ability to bring life to any situation or project. For this case, let us say that the back of this building faces west. This means that once the energy is processed and moves through this building, it has the ability to bring profound change and bring to light the steps for the stable manifestation of reachable goals. Once those steps are completed, or at least are spelled out, then the process starts over again. This will bring you back to the energy of the east when you are again seeking new ideas and fresh energy that will lead to the next steps of working toward your objectives.

Observe the physical features of the landscape that is around your building. The characteristics discussed in chapter 4 now get applied here. Remember that sacred energy flows like water. Trees or other objects directly in front of the front or back entrances can create a blockage or completely choke sacred Power. Is the energy that comes from the street mostly hectic or steady? How much green space is around you and how healthy is it? Is there anything near your space that generates electromagnetic waves or is close to high tension electric cables? What types of buildings are close you? Are there any places near you that contain intense emotions from the past or present, such as a graveyard, hospital, school, or historical location?

Remember to write everything down as you observe your current or potential new space. Whenever possible, find out who was in your space before you and how the space was used. Knowing the history of a location and its surroundings will give you a clue as to the type of ambient energy that you are starting off with.

Next, you will use the Heightening Your Senses exercise, which follows this section, to detect the energetic landscape around your space. Make sure that you do this both indoors and outdoors. Just as I had you take the compass readings more than once, I would ask that you do this exercise at least twice. The reason for this is that you need to make sure that you are in an open, relaxed, and neutral frame of Heart and mind. You need to make sure that your emotions or thoughts are not superseding what your senses are telling you.

Take time to physically walk the perimeter of your property or space with your pendulum and see if there are any ley lines, vortices, or portals. If you need to refresh your memory, refer back to the exercise in chapter 4 on using a pendulum to determine energetic features. Are there any features that you keep being drawn to, such as a tree or a rock? If indoors, are there certain rooms or spots that you keep going back to or feel repelled from? Note what emotions you are feeling. Do you sense if there are nonphysical presences that are watching you? Make sure to write down exactly where you experienced these sensations and what you sensed.

⟡ EXERCISE ⟡
HEIGHTENING YOUR SENSES

This exercise is meant to be done several times at the locations that you frequent. To start the exercise, think about locations that you enjoy in nature and some of your favorite places to go to hang out, eat, or shop. What type of energy do they have? What types of people? What kinds of colors are on the walls?

Evaluate these same questions for places that feel neutral, challenging, or negative. Open your senses and begin to pay attention to what within those environments gives you little to no energy or has negative or toxic vibes. These observations will help you learn to get a baseline of what is around you physically and energetically.

These questions can also be used when you are assessing a property or house that you want to apply the Heart of the Earth method to. In order to fully employ the techniques of the Heart of the Earth, you have to be able to listen to your body, feel if your surroundings resonate with your Heart, and allow for your mind to act as an interpreter. Too many times we are told to rely on what our mind tells us to do. However, you know as well as I do that when we are strictly in our minds, confusion sets in quickly as our minds begin to increasingly chatter on and dismay us with our fears and anxieties, which in turn churns our emotions into a frenzy.

In contrast, our bodies cannot help but *always* live in the present. Typically, it is one of your physical senses that first registers that a place is comfortable and safe, or somehow that something is off and threatening. It is no easy task to ask the mind to take a back seat and allow for your body and your Heart to speak first. Focus special attention to each of your senses one by one. Listen and note what each one of them is telling you. This does not have to be difficult. Once you've done that, think of the sense that is the most pleasurable or is the keenest. Linger within that sense. Begin with that one and then move on to the others one at a time. Do not move on to another one of your senses until you feel that you have received all the information from the one that you were focusing on.

Breathe deeply. Release all the tension in your body. What are the smells that you are noticing at this time and how do they make you feel? Relax your jaw and allow your mouth to open slightly and breathe in slowly through your mouth. What does the air taste like? Notice how the air feels around you and how the land feels beneath your feet. What smells are in the air? Sit quietly and open your mind to absorb what each of your senses is trying to share with you about your environment. What is the energy that you feel around you and how does it affect your own energy and spirit? Stay in this peaceful place of observation. You are training your mind to heed what your body has to say, in addition to listening to the wisdom of your own Heart. I recommend that you do this exercise during the daytime as well as during the night.

For myself, I very much rely on my visual and tactile senses. I also have a very sharp sense of hearing. So when I practice this exercise, I always begin with my sense of sight. I enjoy looking at the sky. I allow my eyes to take in the color of the sky and anything in it, such as clouds or, if it is nighttime, the stars. I then close my eyes and focus my breathing, and with that I begin to direct my focus on my sense of hearing. I listen to the sounds that are around me, both natural and man-made. After taking careful note of what these two senses have to tell me, I then move on to the other three.

STEP FOUR: ASSESSING YOUR RESULTS

After so much preparation, this is the step where all your hard work pays off. It is now time to compare what you have observed about your space against the list of preferences that you made. This will determine the viability of the space in relation to your practical daily requirements and financial parameters. In order to ascertain the spiritual and energetic feasibility, compare what you wrote you needed to feel so your place could be called home to what you recorded when you were walking through the space.

Use the compass points to glance at the innate types of elements and energies that are running through the location in question.

From this comparison, you can decide exactly how much work it would require for this space or property to become what you want it to be. You can decide if the investment of time, energy, and money is worth it in relation to the return you would receive.

Six
PLANNING OUT YOUR SPACE
cx⌒o

Now THAT YOU HAVE determined that a space is going to work for you, the next step is to take a closer look at how to work in harmony with the energies within it. In this chapter, you will learn how to determine the function of a space in relation to the overall feeling that you want to create. I will also teach you how to locate the Heart of your home or work space and how the Arrows of the Medicine Wheel interact with what you are planning. By learning how to overlay the Medicine Wheel on a floor plan, you will see exactly which of the Seven Arrows or Walking Winds watches over a particular room. I will also touch on how to assess if a room needs tweaking if it feels discordant.

STEP ONE:
DETERMINE FUNCTION AND OVERALL FEEL

Setting parameters will act as guidelines as you design a place in alignment with the Heart of the Earth method. You need to determine the purpose and feel of what you wish to create. Also keep in mind the needs of other people and animal companions, if you have them, living with you. How much space do you have to work with? How much space do you need to accommodate everyone? Are you looking at one room or are there several? Is this a private dwelling, rental property, or office location?

Clarifying the overall purpose of the place you are designing is of key importance, for this will determine what you place in the Heart of it. What do I mean by overall purpose? The purpose of a location is defined by considering its functionality. A place for relaxing and recovering from a long day will have a much different feel and look than one made for focusing on work and finishing projects. A place that is crafted for one person will have a unique energy that reflects that individual compared to one that is meant as a gathering place for family, a group of friends, or coworkers. Make sure to distinguish the overall purpose and feel of a space because that will influence how the rooms within it will be designed.

Step Two:
Locating the Heart of Your Space

Locating the Heart of a space can be done one of two ways. The first way is simply finding the exact center of a space. If the space you're evaluating is a single room, get the dimensions of it and draw it to scale on a piece of paper. Grid paper, although very handy, is not necessary. Draw a straight line from one corner diagonally to the one across from it. Repeat with the remaining two corners. It should form an X. The center of the X will show you the physical location of the Heart.

If your place is in an office or home with more than one room, then the process is similar. The difference is that you would measure the overall space that includes *all* the rooms. Once again, draw diagonally from one corner to the other corner to see where the midpoint is. If your place has an irregular shape, like an L, T, or U shape, break it down into rectangular segments and repeat the process. You would have two Xs for potential Heart spaces in the L or T shape. Although the U shape would have at least three Xs (depending on how many segments the U is made up of), the Heart would be dead center at the bottom of the curve. Therefore, when it comes to this shape, only measure the bottom segment that is at the base of the curve. Using this method the X may or may not match up the energetic Heart of a place.

The second method of finding the Heart of a space is observing which room or segment of a space holds the strongest energy. The room or segment with the strongest energy will hold the Heart. How do you determine that? It is not as hard as you think. If a space has a natural energetic Heart, people will unconsciously and continuously gravitate to that spot. You may also find that there is a spot within your space where you feel the most comfortable. You will feel secure, alive, and be able to recharge yourself there.

If you are still uncertain, walk around the space. When you feel yourself attracted to a spot, stop. If you choose to use your pendulum, ask it to point and lead you to where the Heart of your place is. It will pick up intensity in its movements the closer it gets to the Heart. The pendulum will quickly start spinning in a clockwise circle once it is over the exact spot. Make sure that there is nothing around you for about two steps in every direction, then close your eyes. Take a step or two away from that specific spot. Stop. See how that feels and then compare that feeling with the spot where you felt the strongest and warmest energy. If you're using a pendulum, you should notice that when you step away from the Heart, the pendulum will not swing as animatedly as it does when it is exactly over the Heart.

What happens if the location of the natural Heart is not practical? Can the Heart be established in a different place? Yes, it can. I used to live in a place where the energetic Heart happened to be in a very short corridor that connected the kitchen to the family room. You had to go through the family room to reach the bathroom, which was the only bathroom on the lower floor. People used to gather in this tiny corridor all the time and hang out around the peninsula that was there. It was a quite a nuisance because this blocked the entranceway to both rooms and the bathroom. I decided that I needed to set the Heart in a different space instead. I had to channel the energy from the natural Heart to the center of the family room where I wanted family, friends, and guests to spend time together. In chapter 7, I will teach you how to redirect the energy of the natural Heart to establish a new Heart in a different room of your choice. I would like to emphasize that it is always preferable to use the natural Heart of a building instead of creating a different one.

STEP THREE:
OVERLAYING THE MEDICINE WHEEL

Get your drawings of the floor plan of your room, house, or commercial building. Find the exact center of your room or building. You might have already done this step when trying to establish where the Heart of your place will be. Put the center of the Medicine Wheel over the center point of the space. The Medicine Wheel should be drawn big enough so that its circumference will encompass the space that is being evaluated. If you're using the natural Heart spot, observe which direction it lies in. That will be the dominant Arrow that watches over your space. The Arrow's properties and energies will have a strong influence throughout the entire location.

Let us say that after having walked through a house, you sensed that the natural Heart lies in the eastern sector. This means that of the Seven Arrows, it is the spirit of the east that presides over this location and gives it its basic personality. The undertone of this house will be one that welcomes new things and attracts new beginnings. This Arrow likes to create new order and structures that can protect and nurture what is newly born there, whether it be a literal infant or a brand new business. The energy of this sacred Arrow is expansive and likes to bring life and strong energy to whatever it touches. Its personality is kind, just, diplomatic, and demands personal accountability. This Arrow takes into account both the short- and long-term goals before deciding on a course of action. This is a space with an essence of very dynamic but organized energy that will always propel you into the future.

If the Heart of your place coincides with the exact center of your place, then of the Seven Arrows, this is the direction of the Great Spirit. This means that the Power here is universal and open to all expressions. This is the energy and direction of the Creator, meaning all things are possible. Therefore, you could carefully select the essence of the direction you wish to plant in the space and solicit the help of the Arrow that aligns most closely with your intentions to be the dominant energy there.

Although it might be tempting to default to making the Heart the exact center of every place, I strongly caution you against it. Why? To force an unnecessary change of Heart violates the spiritual concept of working in harmony whenever possible. It would be like someone trying to force you to change your personality or behave like someone you are not. Even if you were to entertain this for a short while, ultimately, it would not end well. A location where the Heart was unnecessarily changed requires constant, tremendous maintenance, and if not kept up, will attract sickness and misfortune because the Heart itself will be sick. For you see, the land will continuously fight you to revert back to its natural state.

Observe which compass points are dominant in each room if you are evaluating a space with multiple rooms. It is possible for a room to have more than one energy running through it. Knowing the compass points will graphically show you the types of energy and elements that are most natural in any given place. This is vital information to know when coupling a room with a particular purpose or person in mind. Here you will get an idea of where there already is a natural harmony or potential for discord that needs to be addressed.

GETTING THE ORIENTATION OF ALL ROOMS IN RELATION TO THE MEDICINE WHEEL

If at all possible, get a floor plan of your space. If that is not an option, you can always get grid paper, roughly measure the rooms, and then create a floor plan approximately to scale. If you have more than one floor that you would like to assess, then follow the same procedure for each floor. The reason for this is that you will overlay the Medicine Wheel at the exact middle of the floor plan to get an idea of which Arrow influences an area. Remember to orient the Medicine Wheel in relation to the compass points of the front and rear entrances!

Take extra heed as to where the precise center of your space is, as it could potentially be its Heart. If you can find out exactly when the building was built, this is useful information. The season in which a building is built is another element of its energetic makeup. The season in which something was constructed determines the natural energetic rhythm of a building. At your convenience, use appendix A in the back of the book for a reference list with this information. For now, here is a brief summary of the seasons and their personalities.

- *Spring:* optimistic, provides energy to nurture life, vibrant but gentle and steady.
- *Summer:* enthusiastic, progressive, bold, enhances and accelerates what it touches.
- *Autumn:* pessimistic, quiet yet persevering energy, harvest of efforts.
- *Winter:* conservative, tranquil energy, spiritual and reflective.

Overlay the Medicine Wheel at the exact center of the floor plan and carefully note which rooms fall in which directions. Confirm what compass point the Heart is in if it is not in the dead center of your place, and the direction of the flow of Power, which you assessed by recording the compass points of the front and back entrances of the space. An example of using the Medicine Wheel over a floor plan is pictured in figure 6 on page 128.

This apartment was built in the spring of 1970, which means its natural personality will be optimistic and vibrant but gentle, and have a steady Power that nurtures life. As you can see, the natural Heart of this apartment (located in bedroom A, which is area 5), as indicated by the red heart, is not in a convenient location. The proposed new Heart will be in the living room (this is area 1). The energy of the new Heart will lie in the east. This means that the Arrow of the east will be the sacred spirit watching over this dwelling. The Power of this new Heart comes from and will have the characteristics of the direction of east.

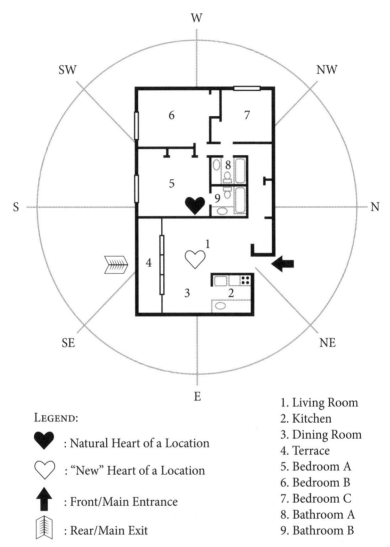

Figure 6: Medicine Wheel over Floor Plan

LEGEND:

♥ : Natural Heart of a Location

♡ : "New" Heart of a Location

⬆ : Front/Main Entrance

📖 : Rear/Main Exit

1. Living Room
2. Kitchen
3. Dining Room
4. Terrace
5. Bedroom A
6. Bedroom B
7. Bedroom C
8. Bathroom A
9. Bathroom B

Remember that the center of your Medicine Wheel *must* be placed over the *natural* Heart of your space! This will guarantee that the compass points are accurately overlaid on your floor plan. Once again, double check to make sure that you have oriented the Medicine Wheel properly in relation to the compass points of the front and rear entrances.

In this example, the front entrance points north. Although this place does not have a back door, the terrace behaves like one and faces south. The Sacred Hoop of this apartment is from north to south and back again. This means that this place attracts the ability for things be completed and then released to open the way to new experiences (north) resulting in expanding new possibilities and going in new directions (south).

I personally like to number the rooms. I like to choose the room closest to the front entrance as area number one and go in a clockwise manner numbering each room in turn until I come back to the front door. Please note that I do not assign a number to the corridors. As you recall, they act as channels for Power to flow throughout a place. If a room is encompassed by more than one direction, then it will default to the most predominant one, as I will explain below. This will show you what type of energy naturally occurs in each room. In the instance of the example in figure 6, this is how I would number and assign the directions of the space:

1. Living room: east. Technically, the living room is encompassed by the directions of east, southeast, and northeast, making the eastern direction predominant.

2. Kitchen: northeast.

3. Dining room: east.

4. Terrace: south. Technically, the terrace is encompassed by the southeast and the south. However, the sliding door, which acts as the rear entrance, opens directly to the south.

5. Bedroom A: southwest.

6. Bedroom B: west.

7. Bedroom C: west.

8. Bathroom A: northwest.

9. Bathroom B: north.

THE COMPASS POINT BY DEGREES

This degree of accuracy is optional, but I am putting this in for those of you who like to get technical. Below is the range that each of the Arrows and Walking Winds of the Medicine Wheel has Power over in relation to the compass points.

- North (0°): from 337.5° to 22.5°.
- Northeast (45°): from 22.5° to 67.5°.
- East (90°): from 67.5° to 112.5°.
- Southeast (135°): from 112.5° to 157.5°.
- South (180°): from 157.5° to 202.5°.
- Southwest (225°): from 202.5° to 247.5°.
- West (270°): from 247.5° to 292.5°.
- Northwest (315°): from 292.5° to 337.5°.

INTERPRETING THE POINTS OF THE COMPASS, THE SEVEN ARROWS, AND MEDICINE WHEEL COLORS

As is true with most cultures, knowing your compass points is important, especially in Native American traditions. These points not only guide you across physical land, they also guide you spiritually and morally. Each of the directions holds a particular energy, represents a stage of life, and has its own color. The associations of the colors I am using are based upon the Anishinaabe Medicine Wheel.

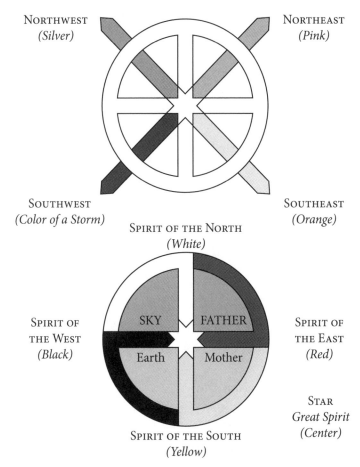

Figure 7: Compass, Seven Arrows, Medicine Wheel Colors

The energy and color correlated with each of the compass points can be introduced into a room as needed. Spirit Keepers watch over the specific compass point that they are affiliated with. They work in harmony with each other and watch over the Medicine Wheel and all that is within it. If an energy goes out of balance and starts creating discord or harm, the Seven

Arrows restore everything back into harmony. If you wish for their blessing to exist in a room that is not in their own direction, you need to ask respectively for that Spirit Keeper to be there. Here is a summary of the colors according to the directions:

- East: red.
- South: yellow.
- West: deepest blue to black.
- North: white.
- Earth Mother (below): green.
- Sky Father (above): sky blue.
- Great Spirit (center): no specific color.
- Northeast: pink.
- Southeast: orange, such as an autumn leaf.
- Southwest: combination of yellow to black, such as a stormy day.
- Northwest: silver gray, such as the moon or a wolf's fur.

East: Dawning of a New Day

The spirit of the east is represented by the color red. Its energy feels like the dawning of a new day. Imagine the sun rising and bringing the fire of life to all of us. This Arrow heralds new beginnings. It represents birth and early childhood. The arrival of a new infant, first day at a new job, or finally taking your first steps into a new venture are a few examples of activities that embody the essence of this compass point. This is the energy that you wish to introduce to the area that might be sluggish. When the energy of the east is out of balance, you will find a person or situation becoming too rigid and feeling as if their standards are the ones the whole world should run by. Another indicator of eastern energy being out of balance is when a person or situation gets stuck in the first steps of a project or problem. Not being able to go beyond the initial stages is very much like a baby who is stuck in a breeched birth position.

The animal that symbolizes this Arrow is the Eagle. The spirit of the east likes to create structures that support the spirit that it houses, very much like your body houses the soul within it or how a business houses the spirit of the dream that it embodies. This divine being assists you in seeing both short-term and long-term impacts of your actions and how they affect everyone and everything in your life.

This Arrow brings new life, revitalizes, introduces new stages of life, and guides you on how to properly navigate these new stages so that they mature into the next stage. This sacred spirit watches over and teaches about divine law, how karma works, and fair laws that we institute in our societies in addition to reinforcing justice. This Arrow's personality can seem stern at first but it is exceedingly fair. Once you get to know east, it brings great inspiration and lifts your dreams, sights, and spirits where they have never been before. If you are willing to discipline yourself to living your purpose authentically, this Arrow can bring in elation like you have never experienced. The Arrow of the east requires that you take the high road and keep in perspective how your actions impact the greater picture of your life and of the world.

South: Spirit of Innocence and Youth

The spirit of the south represents youth and young adulthood. The feeling of the south is similar to when the sun is high and strong in the sky in the summertime. The color of this Arrow is yellow. The south brings growth and assists living beings and projects to develop beyond their initial stages and find their way on the path of life. This is the direction that helps you discover who you are. It is the energy from this compass point that you want to infuse into any situation that needs a new burst of inspiration or high energy. When southern energy is out of balance, it can manifest as self-centeredness, petulant childish behavior, and impulsive foolish actions without thought of the impacts and consequences on themselves and others.

The animal that represents this Arrow is the coyote. This divine spirit brings enthusiastic optimism to any situation and is very daring, sometimes in a foolhardy way. The spirit of the south brings the gifts of innovation, laughter, and a sense of wonder while encouraging you to explore your surroundings and self-expression. The south watches over the follies of youth and the awkward stages of a relationship or project where we are still learning our place within it and how to interact with others. The spirit of this direction teaches us to learn from our mistakes when we fall, to dust ourselves off with good humor, and see how we can approach things in a new way.

The personality of the spirit of the south is the most laid-back of all the directions. The south loves exploration and expanding horizons. It knows when it is time to bend or break the rules. This Arrow loves to laugh at life, to teach you to laugh at yourself and to embrace your inner child. The spirit of the south does have a twisted sense of humor and has no problem throwing you out of your comfort zone or acting in a contrary way to make you go back on your path, if you have gotten lost or confused.

West: Setting Sun and Listening to the Voice Within

The west is the place where the sun goes down. The color that represents this Arrow is the deepest dark blue to black. The west is meant to be a place of rest and reflection, which can sometimes feel scary because you are left to feel as if you are all alone. The stage of life that the west represents is middle age, the point in your life when you have a direction and know how to live your purpose in life. It is the direction of reflecting what has gone on before, learning from it, and thinking into the future for yourself and your loved ones. When in balance, the energy and colors of the west bring rest and allow for deep thought and meditation and healing of the Heart. The energy of this direction also assists with succeeding in your career and building a good reputation in the world.

When out of balance, the colors and directions of the west can bring depression, confusion to your Heart, discord in your relationships, and a conflict between your Heart and mind. Further, when western energy is out of balance, it can manifest as becoming overly withdrawn and completely consumed by fears and worries. Emotions can run into extremes between overwhelming to completely apathetic.

Another way that this energy shows itself when it is out of balance is by being extremely sensitive, to the point where *everything* is personal. The line between you and everyone or everything else becomes blurred beyond recognition. Internal unrest churns to the point where connecting with the outer world seems impossible, pointless, or hopeless.

The animal that represents the spirit of the west is the Great Bear. This animal is extremely powerful and will watch over you just as a mother bear would watch over her cubs. The spirit of the west helps you to heal and recover from deep wounds and trauma so that you can become a whole person again. This Arrow uses a hands-on approach when it comes to teaching.

This Arrow always sends someone to demonstrate and act as a mentor exactly when you need it most and then insists that you put into practice what you have been taught. This sacred Arrow helps you move beyond stagnation and beyond fear, even fear of death itself, to a place of profound inner peace, inner knowing, and deep dreaming to manifest the Heart of the next stage of your life.

North: Path of the Elder and of the Sacred Ancestors

The north is where the sun is at its weakest point of the year. This is when the sun looks like a white disk in the sky. This is the direction that represents elders, moving forward into our golden years, and ultimately our walk back to the Great Spirit when we die. The north represents our time when we are closest to going back to the Great Spirit and when we live so long that our minds go into our "second childhood." It is the Arrow that represents being able to connect with those who have crossed over, including animal companions. This is the direction that represents completion and hard-fought wisdom from living through one's years.

The color of the north, white, helps enhance places devoted to spiritual and meditative practice, the gathering of generations, and places for study, such as libraries, sanctuary rooms, dens, and offices. When the energies of north are in balance, you can see how your wisdom, or information, can be applied in a practical way to create solid foundations of long-term prosperity and stability. When out of balance, north can be a direction that feels life-draining and can cloud the identity of self. Instead of being able to let go and share what you have learned, north, when out of balance, can become a place of stagnation. It can feel like being trapped in a room that has no windows or doors.

The animal that represents this Arrow is the white buffalo. Its personality is like that of a very wise and loving grandmother. The white buffalo is the one who teaches us that life must be both practical and spiritual and because of this we should keep things simple. The spirit of the north is very compassionate, but will not coddle you. Much like a buffalo cow will nudge her calf to get on its feet and get moving, so too will this divine spirit help you get back on your feet when you are lost in the past so that you can move into the next phase of your life or next incarnation. This Arrow watches the sacred path that connects this world and that of the spirit realms of the divine.

Earth Mother: Female Face of the Great Spirit

Earth Mother represents the divine female face of the Great Spirit, and the color of this direction is green. The direction is the ground beneath our feet and represents our internal thoughts and feelings that shape how we perceive the world and how we interact with it, whether we are conscious of it or not. This is a direction that represents the ability to grow many things because it is the direction of fertility, whether it be a desire to grow family, a business, or meaningful relationships.

When the energy of this direction is in balance, it can help with rejuvenation and recovery. Spaces with the energy serve as private places where you can safely reflect, play and experiment, and then assess what resources are needed in order to manifest your plans.

When this energy is out of balance, it becomes all-consuming. It can create energy that leads to unreasonable demands of sacrifice for another purpose or cause, to the point of toxicity and self-destruction. Relationships and situations degenerate into a never-ending pit of commanding *all* of your time, money, and energy, to the extreme point of losing yourself completely. When this energy is out of balance, your world becomes an unwelcoming place where you feel that you are being judged or that you cannot be your true self.

This aspect of the Great Spirit is found in all who are female or embrace a feminine side. The Earth Mother's personality is one of the perfect mother who provides all that is needed for the spirit, body, and mind of her children. She teaches us how to walk gently and respectfully with the natural world and all whom we interact with. This divine spirit shows us how to appropriately manifest what we need and how to responsibly maintain it. She gives us a safe space to become our authentic selves and helps us learn how to express ourselves properly in the outside world. This Arrow shows us how to be compassionate and mindful with all living beings as we walk through life, including ourselves. Earth Mother teaches us how to walk in harmony with the cycles and changes that happen throughout the years.

Sky Father: Male Face of the Great Spirit

Sky Father represents the male face of the Great Spirit and his color is sky blue. His direction is all that is above us. The energy of this direction includes all the dynamic forces and outward expressions of ourselves that we show to the world. When in balance, this energy allows us to feel protected yet aware of changing circumstances around us and know how to respond appropriately to them.

When this direction is in balance there is an easy give-and-take between yourself and others. Communication is clear and manifestations fall into place and are easy to maintain. When the energy of this direction is out of balance, life becomes scattered, chaotic, and consistently erratic. You will find that money slips quickly through your fingers as unexpected expenses hit you, incessant arguments happen through miscommunication, and you have the nagging feeling of not belonging.

This aspect of the Great Spirit is found in all who are male and.those embracing their masculine side. His personality is one of the perfect father who gives us the gifts of oversight, insight, and protection. In Native American teachings, it is said that he teaches us when to listen, when to speak, when to act, and when to be still. Sky Father shows us how to be attentive to the world around us and how to interact with it.

This sacred Arrow guides you to find the balance between your needs and the needs of others. He shows you how to walk courageously in the world as your authentic self without fear and without the need to judge others. Sky Father makes you harness your gifts and engage the energy within you and around you in real time.

Great Spirit: The Creator

This is the direction in the center of the Medicine Wheel. It is also found within your Heart and the Heart of your space. Since the Creator is in all things and beyond all things, there is no specific color that represents the Great Spirit. Therefore, the dominant color or theme is what is whatever is placed in the Heart.

Since the direction of the Great Spirit is the essence of the space you are creating, consider it to be like the physical heart in your body that pumps the blood through to other parts of your body. Whatever you place within the Heart becomes the soul of your place and that energy circulates throughout the rest of your dwelling or work space. This sacred direction sets the mood, energy level, and feeling of a location. Have fun with this direction, for this is where you can express the true essence of what you are trying to create. The energy generated from this direction attracts what you need and repels what you wish to keep away.

This sacred Arrow will guide you unerringly. It is by connecting with the Great Spirit that you can re-center yourself, reconnect the essence of your place, and feel what is needed to restore harmony. Whenever you want to introduce something new that you are unsure of or have a big decision that will have a major impact on all whom you live or work with, connect and meditate with the Heart of your home or work place since this is the place where the Great Spirit resides. You will immediately get an intuitive feedback as to whether your idea is a good one or bad one in the greater scheme of things.

The Walking Winds: The Points Between

The Seven Arrows are points of stability and create a firm sphere of energy. But since this is a world of duality, there also needs to be points of movement. The points between are those points of dynamic, shifting energy. It is simple to remember the colors of the points in between because they are made up of the two colors that are to either side of it. The points between also share the characteristics of the two directions that flank them. Because these are the compass points of perpetual motion, it is necessary to couple them with an Arrow. The Arrow channels the Power of the Walking Winds and gives a stable direction for the energy's movement and an ultimate endpoint.

The Northeast: The Direction of Becoming

Let us start with the northeast. It lies between the white color of the north and the red color of the east. Its color is pink like the blush of dawn just as the sun rises. It represents the stage in life when we are in between lives, such as a baby floating in the womb. This is a direction of infinite potential and of a hopeful future. The energy of the northeast helps to bring warmth and open creativity. When in balance, northeast energy helps promote positive growth and being free of past limitations. The energy of northeast is similar to the initial feeling of disorientation when you take on a new job or a new relationship. You recognize that there is potential, but do not know quite yet what your place is or how to behave. The colors and energy of this compass point help you break free of old limitations and thought patterns.

When out of balance, the energy of this direction is like being stuck in limbo, not knowing which direction is the correct one to walk toward or what to do next. This is why the Power of the northeast is best coupled with an energy that will lead it into a specific direction and goal. This direction assists you to bring in and tap into the energy of infinite possibilities when preparing to enter into a new stage of a project, relationship, or your life at large.

The Southeast: The Direction of Self-Identity

The color that symbolizes the southeast is orange, like an autumn leaf. This direction represents the stage of life when we are between being a small young child and a teenager. The southeast is the direction of self-identity.

When in balance, the energies that are engaged with this direction attract to you people, ideas, and resources that help you to determine who you are and how to proceed in life. When out of balance, southeast energy expresses itself as arrogance, entitlement, and selfishness. An example of this energy is people who act childish and force attention to themselves, which drains time and energy from all who surround them.

The colors and energy of this compass point bring high energy that can be very intense and enthusiastic. Southeast energy can help other energy that is stagnant to flow again and ferrets out old ideas and habits that no longer serve. The Southeast promotes contagious optimism, fun exercise, and enjoyable team building. The energy and colors of this direction are lighthearted and bold.

The Southwest: The Direction of Self-Empowerment

It is hard to describe the colors of this compass point, for they are combination of yellow and black. The colors of this direction are similar to the colors you would see when you look up in the sky and it is becoming stormy. Southwest represents the stage in life that ranges from adulthood to midlife. This is the direction of tremendous Power and the responsibilities that come from wielding it. Whereas the colors and energy of the southeast are bright and lighthearted, the energy and colors of the southwest are more sedate and serious.

The colors of this direction are excellent for business meeting rooms where training takes place or agreements are reached. In a private setting, the energy and colors are perfect for rooms that are used to build deep bonds of family, friendship, and other relationships. These colors promote more mature responses of dedication, commitment, and devotion. The southwest will point out what is relevant to manifest your desires and bring to you what you need to make your mark on the world.

When out of balance, the energy of southwest becomes oppressive or tyrannical. No matter what you do, it will never seem to be enough. Unbalanced southwest energy makes it feel like things never seem to settle down, bringing a feeling that your life has gotten out of control or is no longer your own. It is best to couple this energy with something that brings you joy and support when you need help.

The Northwest: The Direction of Surrender

Northwest is the color of silver gray, like that of the shining moon. The colors of this direction also extend to include metallic colors and pearlescent hues. Northwest represents the stage of life when you are past midlife and heading into becoming an elder. It is that period of time where your children are grown-up and have left home and you wish to streamline your life by removing clutter and old habits, and retiring from jobs or projects you have been involved with. This is the direction of surrendering to the process of change and following through with the transitions that you are calling into your life. This is a place of focus, determination, and actively interacting with the process of transition so that you can bring it to its best possible conclusion.

When the energy of this direction is out of balance, it will manifest as feeling stuck in ruts or as if life is "passing you by" as you lose your sense of purpose and direction. Both are caused by clinging to the past instead of accepting and participating with the changing times. Harnessing the energy of the northwest brings the Power to remove energetic blockages, break through stagnant or stuck situations, and overcome obstacles that can impede life from naturally progressing forward in a healthy way.

DECIDE WHICH ROOMS NEED TWEAKING

As mentioned previously, the natural energetic layout of your property will have areas that are not in perfect alignment with what you are designing a room to become. This is to be expected and is perfectly normal. Analyze which rooms are naturally conducive to what will take place within them or if they need tweaking.

One way of determining this is seeing the natural energy that is in the room in relation to the person or type of activity that the room is supposed to facilitate. This is *very* important because if an energy is converse to the personality of the person who is going to be in a space, there will always be a sense of underlying tension or of something being off. In time, it will have detrimental effects on that person's overall health and well-being.

I will demonstrate two examples. One will require tweaking and the other one will not. Let us say that there is somebody whose personality is one that prefers a very quiet and peaceful environment for their bedroom. The bedroom is located to the south, a place of high energy, which as you could imagine, would *not* be ideal for this person at all! This would definitely be a room that requires adjustments to be made in relation to the naturally occurring energy so that the person can feel at ease in that bedroom instead of at odds.

For the second case, imagine designing a work place and you are trying to decide which room would be a good choice for a team to routinely come together to strategize for the successful conclusion of projects. There is a room facing the southwest, which would naturally have energy and Power conducive for these types of endeavors. This pairing of the proper compass point that the room resides in plus what it will be used for is a powerful and harmonious coupling that creates tremendous potential for financial increase and long-term stability. All that would be needed here would be harnessing the energy so that it would enhance any work done within it.

DOES ANY AREA NEED GRIDDING?

If there is need for ongoing steadying and evening out of the rate of Power streaming onto a property, a building, or a room, it is good to determine grid points. Grid points are places (typically the corners) within a property, building, or room where the element of earth is employed to create a predictable and consistent energy field. Gridding is a form of tweaking the energy of a place so that it becomes more harmonious with what you are designing. I will be talking about how to create a grid in the next chapter. This is an optional step but, I feel, a very valuable one. This is especially good if your place or your entire property is in the proximity of, or *is,* the place where there tends to be hectic activity, or where there is the release of negative or toxic emotions and energy.

Gridding is also used to assist in having two or more energies that are "out of key" with each other to operate more smoothly with each other. Grid points establish points of stability and a field of constant energy that radiates your intention. Grids would be like the stabilizers used on large ships to keep them from rocking as strongly while sailing on an angry sea. I will teach you the simplest form of gridding in the following section on crafting your place.

Seven
STEPS TO CRAFTING YOUR SPACE

❧

WITH ALL THAT YOU HAVE learned so far, it is now time to finally put all of this together to craft your space to be in harmony with the Heart of the Earth! Each of us have different personalities that need to be taken into account when crafting our spaces. Considering others when contemplating how to change your space is very important, in addition to defining what it is that you would like the space to do for you. For example, how we interact with people in a professional situation is vastly different from that of a familiar situation, such as your home or dorm room. If you have animal companions, they also must be included and factored in to determine how the space has to be adapted to ensure that they too may be happy and thrive.

Our spaces are extensions of our bodies and spirit. It is your state of being that creates your circumstances and your environment, not the other way around! Life is a mirror. Everything you see around you is a reflection of your thoughts, beliefs, and emotions that you hold inside, whether you are conscious of them or not. This includes the people you attract into your life, how they treat you, and how they react to the spaces that you create.

⁓ Exercise ⁓
Smudging Ritual: A Simple Ceremony for Blessing and Clearing

Smudging is a traditional Native American technique to bless and clean the energy of items, places, and people. This ancient form of purification, which calls in the Seven Arrows, is always done before the undertaking of any task. Smudge is made of specific herbs to accomplish this. The combination of herbs that I prefer is cedar, sage, and sweetgrass. Although these herbs are typically burned to produce the desired effect, they can also be just as effective when turned into a liquid holding the essential oils of the plants. This is especially useful if you have someone with respiratory issues or are in an environment where smoke is prohibited.

Here's what you'll need for the ritual:

- Smudge stick, which can consist of bundled herbs or essential oils. The herbs or oils can be purchased online from reputable holistic vendors.
- A feather for fanning the smudge to the Seven Arrows. A turkey or goose feather is the most common.
- A shell or other fireproof container to hold a burning smudge stick.
- A compass to determine where the four cardinal points are (optional).

The ritual of smudging is performed the same way whether smoke or liquid form is used. If using the liquid form of smudge, create a misting spray with the oils and water. Spray the mist into the air and use the feather to waft the mist in the direction that it's supposed to go. If you are burning smudge, make sure that you have the windows cracked or that the place has good air circulation so that the smoke does become too dense and can dissipate quickly.

Steps for Smudging

- Begin by smudging yourself plus any tools or items that you will be using.
- Look to the south and offer the smudge to the spirit of the south by wafting the smoke or mist in that direction four times. Give thanks to this sacred Spirit Keeper for coming to help you.
- Turn ninety degrees to your right so that you are facing west. Repeat the previous step, but offer the smudge to the spirit of the west.
- Turn ninety degrees to your right so that you are facing north. Offer the smudge to the spirit of the north.
- Turn ninety degrees to your right so that you are facing east. Offer the smudge to the spirit of the east.
- Turn ninety degrees to your right so that you are again facing south, then turn toward the center. Fan the smudge to the ground to offer to Earth Mother.
- Look up to the sky and fan the smudge to the heavens or to the ceiling to offer to Sky Father.
- Fan the smudge over yourself and whatever is in the center to honor the Great Spirit.

• If using a smudge stick extinguish it thoroughly. You are now ready to begin your project. You only need to smudge once before you begin working every day.

Important note: If you were burning the smudge and after you make sure that it is properly extinguished, you *must* bury the ashes or offer them to the winds. Returning the ashes of the herbs back to Earth Mother honors the spirit of the plants that gave themselves for your prayers. From a practical standpoint, the ashes of these herbs act as nourishment for the next generation of plants. This completes a Sacred Hoop.

ESTABLISHING THE HEART OF A PLACE

This is one of the most critical steps in this entire process of crafting your space! Please do not rush this step for the Heart of your space will hold its essence and its health for the duration that you are there. Determine whether you will be using the natural Heart of your space or one that you establish. It is best to use the original Heart whenever possible. It will allow for the innate rhythms of your space to flow naturally with the greatest benefit to you and those who are there. However, sometimes it is necessary to move the Heart of a place, which we'll discuss in the next section. This can happen when the natural Heart is in a location that is extremely inconvenient or hazardous.

Getting back to using the existing Heart, once you have determined where it is, choose an item that will symbolize the essence of what you are creating and place the item in the exact center of your space. Focus your energy and your feelings while touching the item and concentrate on the qualities that you would like the Heart to hold. Think of different blessings you would like for yourself and for those who will be there with you, such as strong health, prosperity, or love. Envision the item filling up with the energy of the blessings and awakening a heartbeat within it. Imagine the heartbeat becoming stronger and radiating the energy, your intentions, and blessings within it.

After you have completed this process, you may carefully select where you will place the item, as it is the anchor piece of your space. I would like to emphasize that the anchor piece does *not* have to be the focal point of the room. The item that holds the essence of the Heart merely needs to be present somewhere within that room.

Method for Establishing a New Heart

There are extra steps to do if you are going to create a new Heart for your space instead of using the original one. In a way, the term "new" is misleading for what you are doing. You're not creating a new Heart but merely channeling the energy from the natural Heart to another space where you wish for the heartbeat to be strongest.

For this, you will need two anchor pieces, rather than just the one used in the previous section. The first step is to find the center of the room or space that holds the natural Heart as well as the place you would like to create the new one. Use common sense and safety if the natural Heart is not in a safe location to reach. If you can't safely reach the Heart, get as close as you reasonably can to it.

Once you've reached the Heart, choose which of your two items will remain in the original location of the natural Heart and which will anchor down the other end of the energetic bridge as you are establishing the new Heart. The items do not have to be identical, but they should be similar in theme since the physical link of energy is more powerful when you do this.

Bless both spaces and the items by calling in the Seven Arrows with a smudging ceremony. Take both items to the room or space where the natural Heart is located and once again focus on filling both of them with the energy of the natural Heart as well as envisioning infusing the items with the blessings that you would wish for you and those who live with you.

Walk only the item that is to be the anchor for the channeled energy from the natural Heart to the center of the desired room that is to be the home for the new Heart. Envision and feel the energy flowing freely and strongly from the natural Heart to the anchor item in your hands. It is vital that you take time to feel and envision the flow from the natural Heart to the new one that you are creating. The essence that the Heart will circulate will only be as strong as the effort you put into creating it! Place the anchor item for the new Heart somewhere in the space where you are moving it.

The other item will remain somewhere in the space where the original Heart is. Please note that the channel between the two rooms should always be kept clear! It does not mean that the two places have to be in a straight line, but the corridor or rooms in between them should be kept free of obstacles, similar to the idea of keeping the arteries of your human heart clear for better health.

THE IMPACT OF COLOR

On the topic of colors, I will bring only the most basic and general of tips. I am not an interior designer, but I will give you the bare essentials so that you may be successful in creating a place that will make you and others with you happy. Color is all around us and it affects our moods and energetic levels, whether we are conscious of it or not. Colors are used all the time to influence us. You see this when you are enjoying a movie where the scene might be humorous and light, or mysterious, dark, and foreboding. Colors are constantly used in marketing to try to catch your eyes and sway your feelings and opinions about a product.

Here are some general rules of thumb so you can get a rough idea as to how to choose your colors and how to apply them. Warmer colors can inspire energy and enthusiasm. Warm colors include red, orange, yellow, or pink. Avoid using warm colors in small spaces, as they can make a space feel closed in. Cool colors, on the other hand, instill calm and will help you focus. In the work space, cool colors speak of professionalism. Cool colors in a large room will make it appear even larger and can create a disconnected, stark, and unwelcoming feeling much like being lost in an impersonal place like an institution. Examples of these types of colors include blue, green, and purple. Shades of white tend to open up space. Using gray colors will help to make things seem more businesslike and sophisticated, and have a sharper look.

Colors can be used to your advantage. If you have a space that is small, then using a cool color that is lighter will make a room feel safe and a little larger. On the other hand, a color that is darker will make a place appear smaller. This knowledge can assist with making a smaller space appear roomier or a larger space a bit cozier. For a very large room a warmer color that is darker or more intense can be painted on one wall to act as an anchor wall that draws attention and will act as a natural gathering point. An anchor wall in a large space makes a room feel more grounded because it gives it a point of orientation, and therefore makes it more comfortable.

When choosing colors, it is best to have a dominant color with other complementary ones alongside it to make a room feel complete and more interesting. This is not only for aesthetic reasons. The dominant color acts as a foundation that steadily holds the type of sacred Power you want in a room. I would ask you to consider two factors when deciding on a dominant color. One of them is the Medicine Wheel. Please use the Medicine Wheel color chart in figure 8 to establish the type of sacred Power and element you want in that room.

What you select as the primary Power needs to be represented in the space in some way, such as a piece of decor if it is not to be the dominant color. Another thing to consider is how a color makes you feel both emotionally and energetically. Both of these factors are equally important! Once you have decided which color will be dominant, use a standard color wheel to locate your dominant color and see the color options that will accompany it.

I will mention four methods to assist you in choosing your color scheme. Please know that the internet can go into further detail, or if you prefer, consult someone who is trained in interior design.

Complementary Colors

Complementary colors are opposite each other on the color wheel, such as blue and orange. You would select one of them to be the predominant color and the other as an accent. The contrast can be rather striking. You must use a neutral color to help bring harmony by acting as a bridge between the two complementary colors. For example, I could choose to paint a room a sky blue color and have the trim be silvery white of summer clouds. Then I could choose decorations or an item in that room that is a variation of the color orange. Blue and orange are complementary, silvery white is the neutral bridge between them.

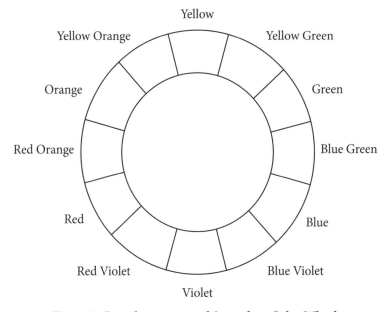

Figure 8: Complementary and Secondary Color Wheel

Complementary Combinations

Another way to combine colors is through a complementary combination. This is a great way for beginners to choose colors for a room because it naturally lends itself to a greater harmony. A complementary combination is when you choose one color to be dominant and, instead of choosing the complementary color directly across from it on the color wheel, you choose the two colors next to its complementary color. Say, for example, you choose blue and to either side of its complementary color, which is orange, are the colors yellow orange and red orange. If I paint the room to be a sky blue color, I would choose my trim and baseboards to be a neutral color. Wherever I would like to draw the eye, I could put accent pieces, such as pillows, that would be yellow orange and red orange. Use both the complementary and split complementary combinations when you really want a vivid contrast that pops.

Triadic

The third combination of colors is called a triadic. This is when you skip an equal number of spaces between three colors to make a combination. A combination could include red, violet, and orange; or blue violet, blue green, and yellow green.

Analogous

The fourth and final way to create color combination is called analogous. This combination occurs when you choose three colors that are side by side, such as yellow, yellow orange, and orange. When using this form of combining colors, it is best to keep cool colors with cool ones and warm colors with warmer colors, unless you have a *very* good idea of how to use colors. The best way to manage this combination is to choose a dominant color and have the others serve as accent colors.

PROPER USE OF LIGHT

Just as color can help to influence our emotions, lighting also has a profound impact on our energy levels, attitudes, and perceptions. The reason is that light affects our circadian rhythms. These rhythms are the natural cycles in our bodies that affect our mental and physical behaviors, as well our personal energy levels throughout the course of a day.

Because of this, light is a *very* important aspect to ponder when crafting your space. The amount of light in your environment will have an impact on your overall mood and well-being.

It will amplify or diminish the effects of the colors you put into a room. Reflect upon how you feel more upbeat during months when there is more sunlight, such as the spring and summer. Conversely, you may find yourself feeling more sluggish or depressed when it becomes darker for longer stretches of time during the fall and winter.

Whenever possible, natural lighting is always preferable as it shows the true colors of the items that you are putting into a room and the paint on the walls. If you find that there is little natural light or there are no windows, it is better to install light bulbs that mimic natural light in the places you tend to be in the most.

Beyond helping you remain in a good mood, another reason to keep your spaces well lit is that insufficient lighting can make a small room feel even smaller and very cramped. Imagine a small room after it is full of furniture and is dimly lit. It can feel like the walls are closing in on you and you are going to be smothered alive in that place. Fortunately, technology has advanced beyond incandescent light bulbs so that there are good selections of different types of lighting, keeping both our planet and your budget happy.

Think about what feeling you want a room to have in relation to its function in order to decide if you should go with bright or gentle light. Brighter lights will help you to focus. They are often the choice for places that require consistent concentration and intensity for prolonged periods of time, such as a work place, a medical or educational institution, or a sports facility. Would you like help eating less to stick to your diet? Install a bright light where you eat. You will find yourself eating more deliberately and eating lighter meals. Restaurants use soft lighting, which makes you relax. The more you relax, the longer you will linger. The longer you linger, the more you will eat and drink. Putting brighter lighting into a space subconsciously gives you the message that you need to focus on finishing your meal so that you can move on to your next set of tasks.

If you wish to create a cozier space, then gentle lighting is preferable. Soft lighting makes it easier to release tension and creates a sense of safety for your spirit, body, and mind. It is the ideal choice of lighting in a bedroom, meditation space, or recreational room. It can also help a huge space seem less intimidating by making it feel smaller.

Because I want to live in harmony with nature's cycles, as well as of those of my body, I have different types of bulbs in my house that produce both bright and soft lighting. I have put several LED bulbs in my ceiling lamp where I work and full spectrum lights throughout my home since I don't have dimmer switches. It gives me the option to create bright light when I need to work, and as I grow tired as the day goes on I back it down to soft light to help me to relax. This does wonders to improve my mood and enhance my energy levels, even on the darkest of days! Be aware that LED and compact fluorescent bulbs produce a significant amount of blue light, which can interfere with sleep.

MAKING A SMALL SPACE SEEM BIGGER

One of the most impactful ways to make a small space seem larger is to find ways to spread light around and soften corners and recesses of the room when illuminating them. You can visually create a larger space with corner lamps, wall sconces, or a bright central hanging light. The idea is to draw the eye vertically and upwards with your lighting. In a small space, drawing the eye horizontally will make a room seem much smaller. You can also use mirrors to reflect more light into your room.

Another impact on the size of a space is that the furniture has to be in proportion to the room. For a small space, use one large piece of furniture, or two at most, which either go wall to wall or ceiling to floor. This can trick the eye in making a room appear larger. In addition, I also recommend using pieces of furniture that are low to the ground and that show their legs. A room seems airier if you use sleek furniture versus big, heavy pieces. If you absolutely feel the need to use a heavy piece as a focal point for the room, a work of art hanging on the wall would be a good choice. I personally prefer multifunctional furniture. In my small space, I have a futon that has drawers underneath to store of blankets and pillows.

A small space benefits from the use of reflective and shiny surfaces. Placing a mirror strategically so that it reflects the natural light of the room will fool the eye into making a room seem much larger than it is. These surfaces create a sense of openness and brightness, which makes a room feel lighter and more spacious.

Make sure that you create paths so that movement is easy throughout the space. If necessary, you can group your furniture to one side of the space. The idea is if you can move freely throughout the room without bumping into something, it gives the impression and sensation that the room has ample space. Another idea is to use either no drapes or breezy fabrics on the windows to avoid visually separating the room. Of course, we all have the need for privacy so the use of some blinds may be necessary.

Getting storage that is appropriate for your needs is mandatory in a small space. Think beyond the present and calculate how much more storage space you might need as you accumulate more possessions. As I mentioned before, furniture that has built-in drawers or storage bins is perfect if you have a small home or work space. In addition to making your place look tidy, it is very convenient to have what you need within hand's reach at all times. Although this might not seem like an important piece of advice, leave some empty space on any shelves instead of cramming them with things. When you leave space, it subconsciously gives the message that there is room for expansion.

The key to making a small space seem bigger is to use many different elements to reinforce a sense that the space is open and airy. You will definitely feel that you have room to breathe and stretch. It makes all the difference between a space that feels open and entices you to snuggle down and get comfortable versus a space that feels full and like you are huddled in a tiny cave.

MAKING A BIG ROOM SEEM SMALLER

If you find that a room is so large that it feels more like a ballroom, here are some tips to help you make it cozier. First off, small furniture in a large room only helps to exaggerate how large the room is. Whatever furniture you choose should be in proportion to the size of space. In a big space, large furniture, such as a long sofa or large area rugs, can help the room feel more manageable. Short bookshelves or cabinets help to lower the ceiling in a big space. Another trick is using corner furniture, like a table or a corner shelf. When placing furniture in a large space, keep it away from any walls. Putting something closer to the center of your space and away from walls draws attention to the furniture and makes it serve as a centerpiece.

In many modern home floor plans, it is more common to find an open floor design, rather than a design of small rooms. For spaces with large, open floor plans, it's best to break that space down into two or three smaller areas that have different activities.

For example, one portion of the space could be used as a recreational area where you can unwind and watch movies. That area could be furnished with a big sofa that has nice fluffy pillows, perhaps even a fireplace. The other portion of the room could be used as a sitting area where you put a round table with straight-backed chairs. This would break up this large space into two "rooms," one for enjoying a relaxing activity and the other for sitting more attentively to do work or engage in conversation.

In a large space, you also need to pay attention to colors. The lighter the color, the larger and more open a space will seem. Using darker and less reflective colors will make a large space look smaller. If you wanted to use a green color in a big space, selecting a rich forest green instead of a light mint cream hue would be the proper choice. You could achieve a similar effect with wallpaper that has subtle but large patterns.

I should emphasize that you *must* use good lighting! This way the dark colors will bring a richness to the space. Dim lighting will make your space appear overly dark and depressing like a cavern. Also, shy away from shiny and reflective surfaces in large space. Instead use a matte or eggshell finish with paint. Incorporate wood or stone because they are grounding elements and they also subconsciously give the message that the space is cozier than it really is.

Just as the furniture needs to match the size of the room, the decorations should also be equal in scale. Always use larger decorations or paintings in large spaces. As you hang works of art or decorations, remember to place them lower to create a horizontal line. As the eye follows the horizontal line, it helps to create a subconscious idea that the ceiling is lower and the room is not quite as large.

SECONDHAND ITEMS

Everything around us absorbs the influence and intensity of our moods and the emotions generated by our activities. Because of this, I strongly urge that if you buy objects from a secondhand shop, you perform a cleansing smudge ritual on them before using them, including items gifted to you from a friend or relative. This will be *especially* true for those of you who are empaths!

I remember an acquaintance who purchased an old Victorian-style dresser from a secondhand shop. Shortly after the dresser was moved into his home, he started seeing the shadow of a man. Although this ghost never did anything alarming, it would frighten him terribly. He contacted me because of this new haunting, and as a part of the work, I asked him to inquire about the history of the dresser. He discovered that this piece of furniture was from an estate and belonged to a man who had died alone. Once I performed a cleansing ritual and said a prayer to ask the spirit of the former owner of the dresser to have a safe journey back to the Creator, everything went back to normal.

Any item, whether it be clothing, furniture, or even a decoration, can carry more than just the dust and physical remnants of the past. In order to clean the objects, you need to bless them with smudge and offer the item back to the Creator. If the item can be wiped down without ruining it, make a mixture with a couple drops of lavender oil, or a combination of sage and cedar oils, with a cup of water. Make sure that you buy essential oils and not fragrance. Washing your item down with this gentle solution smells very pleasant and will eliminate any energetic residue that remained from previous owners.

It is wonderful to use items over again. I have found many treasures by going to secondhand shops, antique and curiosity stores, and garage sales. However, sometimes bargains, if you are not careful, can come with a bigger price than you anticipated.

How to Set the Dominant Energy in a Space

As mentioned previously, you can see the energy of a space by noting which compass point it falls in and how that direction relates to the Medicine Wheel. The energy is also influenced by the people who will be in the space most of the time, the purpose for which the space is being created, and potentially by spirit forces or divine forces, if you are introducing Them into a space.

The natural sacred undercurrent is the Power that will be ever present and ever influential, regardless of what will go on in this particular space. Anything you put in that room will be like a boat that is in a flowing stream or ocean bay. Yes, an anchored boat would remain in the same approximate location, but it will turn in relation to the current or tide. If not secured, the boat would aimlessly drift. The same can be said for a room that does not have a focus. In order to enhance the energy that you wish to be dominant in a space, you need to introduce items that anchor that energy and use colors that will represent the element that you want to bring in.

The most harmonious arrangement is to have a room's function follow the natural energy that is within it. If you wish to enhance the naturally occurring Power, introduce items or colors that bring in the energy of its opposite compass point in order to complete a Sacred Hoop of Power. This idea is similar to understanding the flow of energy between the front and rear entrances of a space if they are across from each other on the compass. This helps to create a miniature current of energy that will feel the most in alignment with the natural world.

Let us say that my goal is to design a room for writing and creativity. The room that I have available is aligned to the southeast. This is an ideal placement because southeast is a point between, which is a direction of moving energy. More specifically, the direction of southeast represents the Place of Self-Identity through the development of self-expression and creativity. If I wanted to reinforce the influences of the southeast, I would choose colors that represent it in some way. For example, I might place a bronze dragonfly on the wall. The dragonfly represents quick movement, piercing through illusions, and the transformations in life that come through living in truth. I might also add some room accents in harvest colors, like red, orange, or yellow. But since I would also like for my efforts to come to completion, I want to introduce elements that represent the compass point opposite of southeast.

The direction opposite the southeast is the northwest. The northwest is the Place of Surrender. Surrender, as taught to me by my Seneca Medicine Teachers, means owning and fully participating in the process of change and transformation from beginning to end. This is the perfect compass point for this purpose. So many times it is tempting to start things but never finish them. Introducing the energy of the northwest helps to complete the circle with the southeast. For this purpose, I may add highlights of silver in a space to represent the direction of northwest.

In this example, I also want divine masculine energy, so I may paint the room sky blue. From a psychological standpoint, it lifts my morale because the color mimics that of the sky on a beautiful, perfect day. The energies of the southeast and northwest work in harmony and enhance the influence of the undercurrent. I created a room like this in real life and having the energy come full circle has aided me tremendously in becoming an author and completing countless other important tasks in my life.

Whenever you introduce representations of a compass point that is opposite of your dominant one, it helps to complete a Sacred Hoop. Imagine that each space is like its own miniature Medicine Wheel. Completing the circle is harmonious with nature, since nature is a series of cycles. If you wish to review this topic again, please go back to chapter 3 under Interaction of the Elements among the Four Cardinal Points.

Time to focus on another example. Let us say that you want the dominant energy of a space to revolve around the intended function of it. Pretend that the space is located in the northeast. You would like the function for this room to be your private meditation space to find inner peace after a hectic day. As you recall, the energy of northeast is that of a Place of Becoming, which is infinite potential. This compass point is a place of discovery, but of no final concrete form.

In some ways, designing a meditation space with this energy is useful, but not ideal. It is not conducive to being able to go more deeply into your center and your meditations to find tranquility and answers to your questions. The points in between, like northeast, are compass points of constant movement, which are hardly restful for a meditation room. You need a source of energy to act as a stable foundation. You would do this by introducing one of the four cardinal directions: north, south, east, or west. For a meditation space, you'd need energy for finding solutions and transforming situations to the best possible outcome, which would be aligned with the direction of west. The compass point of west is a point of stability. It is the direction of the element of water and of the Heart.

Since this space will be for your use only, you need symbols representing and honoring the sacred beings that you walk with, plus any items that help you focus while you meditate. It would also be helpful to add personal comfort items, such as pillows or a comfortable meditation chair. These personal items should be sufficient to honor the western energy that you bring into the mix because these things are sacred in your Heart. If you wanted to request the blessings of the spirit of the west (Bear) specifically, you would put items in the space that honor and invite this divine being in, such as images or paw prints of the Bear, or stars to symbolize the night sky.

In this example, you are setting the predominant energy of this space to that of the west and the element of water. There is no harm in doing this because the undercurrent of the northeastern energy would have a tendency to leave things open-ended instead of giving closure or completion. This constant undercurrent of the northeast would drive things to be more superficial, which would work against you if your goal is to go more deeply with meditations and studies. To makes things smoother, you could also introduce another element, like spirit. Spirit would have a double benefit in this particular instance since your space would be intended as a place of meditation and spiritual study.

As a rule of thumb, when there are two forces that do not work easily or naturally with each other, such as this example, it is important to introduce the element of spirit, which is in the center of the Medicine Wheel and the place of the Great Spirit. The element of spirit acts as a balance point and a buffer so that the two potentially discordant energies can work hand in hand. Since the center of the Medicine Wheel is the place of the Great Spirit and it is a neutral force, it has no limitations when it comes to being represented. Any color representation is possible. This element acts as an intermediary between *all* points.

As such, it acts as a peacekeeper amongst all the elements and energies. If you wish to have more of a masculine energy, you would introduce colors or items that represent Sky Father. If you wish to bring in more of the divine feminine force, you would bring in items and colors that enhance Earth Mother's influence.

In this case, you would choose a color that symbolizes the Creator. You could choose accent items or pillows with an off-white color that have the slightest blush of lavender. It would also be helpful to select items and symbols to represent the colors and energies of water. Since you do not wish to enhance the natural energy in this room, do not place anything that would amplify the energy of the northeast. For example, you would not paint this room with pink since it could enhance northeast energy.

Finally, add the colors or items that represent your own personal Good Medicine. These are items that reflect your talents and way of being. If this were my room I would add accents of the color of Aztec gold. This is one of the colors that represents the Fire Eagle Medicine that I carry. I would also have an image of a Fire Eagle.

A final option for setting predominant energy of a space is to choose the energy of a person to be dominant. Let us say that the person in question is an individual who has quiet energy and is very serious, but the room that they have faces south. The element of this space is air and the Arrow of the south is one of high energy. This Spirit Keeper watches over the essence of youth and is very lighthearted.

For someone who needs a peaceful environment of stillness and quiet, this would be equivalent to them going to a stadium where everyone is wildly cheering because their favorite soccer team just won the FIFA World Cup! Colors that should be considered to calm this room could be either those of the west or the north, since both of these directions hold more introversive and tranquil energy. The aspects of the southern energy would need to be significantly calmed down. The easiest and most natural way to do this is by bringing in the energy of its complementary compass point to form a Sacred Hoop. Here, it would be important to introduce elements and energies from the north.

The Arrow of the north is a place of tranquility and speaks of maturity and moving in a stately way, which can be brought about as a result of properly channeling the rapid excitement of the south. To bring in the energy of the north, that person would place elements of earth or some kind of heirloom in that room. The reason for this is that the energy of the spirit of the north represents the wisdom and stately pace of an elder. This compass point holds the element of earth. Completing this Sacred Hoop of Power, that of young energy touching the energy of the old and back again, allows for any events that take place in that room to move from beginning to end in a harmonious, peaceful flow. Under these circumstances, the energy from the south should not be amplified at all.

The rule of thumb is that it is preferable to complete Sacred Hoops whenever possible so long as the resultant energy is the type that you desire. Sacred Hoops formed from the cardinal points will produce a foundational energy that you can build upon. Sacred Hoops created by the Walking Winds (the points between) will result in a current of energy that promotes perpetual movement and change.

What to Do with Pockets of Stagnant Energy in Your Home

Just as there are places of movement, there are also places of stillness within any space. Observe the areas in your home or work place where the flow of sacred energy moves sluggishly or comes to a standstill. The feeling of stagnant energy is similar to being by a river or stream where there are odd pockets of still water along its edge. The same can be said to be true of a building. You will notice that there are places where things tend to accumulate, are forgotten, or act as a clutter magnet. The remedy for those areas where there is stagnant energy is putting something there that will anchor and strengthen one of your intentions. When you do this it converts this dead space to one of stability with a purpose.

Imagine there is a house where the front entrance faces the northeast, which on the Medicine Wheel is the direction of becoming (infinite potential). The rear entrance points southwest, which on the Medicine Wheel is the direction of the power of storm (catalytic forces) and self-empowerment. There is a poorly lit hallway that meanders through the house and joins the front and the back doors. In one of the nooks, created where the corridor changes direction, is a place of stagnation.

Instead of allowing an ever-growing pile of clutter that you promise to get back to later (but never do), place a physical item that is a symbol or the embodiment of a blessing or concept that you want to take root. Maybe you wish to focus on one aspect of your happiness, like developing a healthy balance between family life, or attracting prosperity, such as growing your career. To represent a tight-knit family, you could put a picture or reminder of your family.

However, you also want to anchor opportunities for prosperity and abundance to consistently be brought into your home. After all, there are always bills to pay, right? To represent that idea, you could put a stone there that has the word prosperity on it. Note that for the aspects of work and abundance, I place something made of stone because stones are considered to be the bones of Earth Mother. They embody the earth element, which is an element that creates consistent energy and attracts practical resources for building upon for years to come.

For the representation of family, I would recommend an image or a figurine made of a substance other than stone to bring in another element and feeling. Stone can be very cold, which is not the mood you would want for your relationships with your family! Because of this, your representation of family needs to give you, and anyone who gazes upon it, a heartwarming and comforting feeling.

With an anchor set, the sacred Power of the space will no longer get stuck in this spot and will flow along. It will swirl through this eddy and as it does so the Power becomes filtered so that what begins to be diffused throughout your house is an even stronger expression of your current goals.

Harnessing Energetic Features

Now is the time to refer back to your notes from when you used your pendulum to determine the energetic features—ley lines, portals, or vortices—of your place. If you would like to double check your findings, you can refer back to chapter 4 if you need to remember how to do the steps and how to interpret them.

I would like to mention some basic characteristics that pertain to all energetic features regardless of what they are. Since ley lines, portals, and vortexes are connected beyond this three-dimensional world, they can behave independently of the land. For example, a ley line flowing from north to south does not automatically carry the blessings of the Spirit of the South. You need to feel and/or ask your pendulum as to what type of energy that this ley line would hold. You can also ask your spirit guides. To make it easier, you can ask using the energy types based on the Medicine Wheel to get an idea as to the quality of the energy that flows within that specific ley line.

You also have the option of leaving these features alone if they are not interfering with you. The less that you interfere with nature, the better it is for everyone. In Native American traditions, a fundamental principle is to work in respect and harmony with the land as much as possible and not impose upon it unless absolutely necessary. However, it is okay to harness a ley line, portal, or vortex if it will affect you or those who share your home or work space. This is especially true if the energy is draining, discordant, or toxic.

It is paramount that you understand that the essential characteristics of an energetic feature *cannot be changed by mere human beings.* In other words, you cannot convert a portal into a ley line or a vortex. You would not be able to change the innate direction, flavor, or strength of the flow of the sacred energy moving through this energetic feature.

If you're relaxed and receptive while evaluating the energetic features of your space, your senses often become enhanced and it is common to be able to feel the strength, direction of the flow of sacred energy, and the overall feel of the energetic feature in question. You may also receive suggestions from the land itself as to what it prefers or needs in order to hold your intentions so that the sacred energy runs smoothly. It would also help for you to determine the boundaries of the area you are working on by trusting your body's senses or to use your pendulum to see the boundaries. If you still feel that unsure of your results you could always hire a professional geomancer such as a shaman, or a dowser to confirm your findings.

Before empowering an object to harness an energetic feature, place it in the area of the energetic feature. Feel if the energies enhanced by the object are compatible or if there is resistance. If you feel any discord between the object and the energetic feature, try a different object. Let the land speak to you. Once you find the object that will work in harmony with the land and in alignment with your intention you will need to follow the same process to bless and empower the item like you did when establishing the Heart of your space earlier in this chapter. The only difference is that this will only affect the specific ley line, portal, or vortex that it is connected to and it will not interfere with the Heart of your place. As a reminder, never put a picture of a person in any type of energetic feature, as it may accidentally and detrimentally affect their lives and their health. That being said, let's move on to how to uniquely handle each energetic feature.

Ley Lines

After ascertaining the strength of flow, direction, and type of energy of a ley line, you can now choose how to interact with it. Pay attention to the rooms it moves through. If the type of energy is agreeable, you can leave it alone, dampen, or enhance its effects. For example, let's say the energy is able to help you recharge and runs through the family room, the hallway, and a bedroom before going back outside. Remember that ley lines are like streams. This means that you don't have to put an object to enhance or adjust the ley line's energy in every room, you could simply put it in the family room where the stream will pick it up and it will naturally flow into the other rooms. In this particular example, this type of energy might be too active for a good night sleep, and I would suggest placing a grounding item, such as wood, stone, earth, or plants, to help soften or ground the energy.

If the energy of the ley line is not conducive to what you want, it would need to be dampened or redirected. Again, the vision of a stream is very useful here. Remember that a ley line is a force of nature and it cannot be dammed up without severe and potentially punishing results. Let's pretend that the energy from this particular ley line is one of breaking things down. It runs through an office, a bathroom, and a lounging area. You could leave it alone for the bathroom. But for an office or lounging area, this can go against what you're trying to achieve. In the office space, you can redirect this force and ground it by using a stone or grounding crystal. The stone or crystal would push this energy field back into the earth where it would resurface in the next room. You could use the same strategy for the lounging room, but I would offer another suggestion. There is nothing wrong with using this "breaking down" energy in a lounge space to let go of tensions, anger, or frustrations. Here you could use one of the colors or symbols of the west in the ley line to enhance it, since the west holds the power of transformation. You can set the intention of breaking down toxic emotions so that people become liberated from them and feel better when they leave the lounging space.

Portals

As discussed earlier, portals can be thought of as doorways that can swing either in one direction or two. If you feel there is a draft in your space that moves away from you, it means there is a portal that opens into the spirit world and moves spirits and energy from this world into that realm. If you feel a draft blowing over you, similar to opening an outside door leading into your house, that means there is a portal bringing energy or spirits from the spirit world to this one.

Portals are natural passages between our world and other spiritual realms. The majority of portals are benign and helpful and can be left alone with no ill effects. If you do not feel secure with a portal because you are unsure of what will be moving through it, you may dedicate it to a specific purpose. You can attune a portal so that only specific beings have access to it or so only a specific type of energy can flow through it.

If the portal is outward bound, meaning the energy flows from our realm into the spirit realms, you may place an item or color that represents what you wish to have removed from your home or space. I have one such portal where I placed a small statue of a gargoyle that was gifted me by a friend to help escort any toxic or chaotic energies that could cause illness or ill fortune to me and those of my household. Because I live in an apartment complex, the energy around me can be mostly good but unpredictable due to the wide variety of people who live around me. In order to be respectful of the spirit realms, (they are not a dumping grounds after all) I've asked the gargoyle to escort this energetic trash to where it needs to go so that it harms no one else.

If the portal in your space is inward bound, meaning the energy flows from the spirit realms into ours, you may place an item or color the represents a guardian that you want watching over the portal, or energy or spirit beings that you would welcome in your home. A strong note of caution: if you invite spirit beings, stick to beings of the highest order, such as gods and goddesses, ascended Masters, or angels. Please only invite spirit beings if you are experienced or are familiar with the beings.

I personally feel that it is an intelligent practice to ask a guardian to watch over a portal that is inward bound and put a representation of that guardian at the location of the portal. In addition to the guardian, you may also place anything around the portal that represents the blessings or energies you would like for the portal to usher into your home.

If the portal is inward bound and is bringing energy or spirits that are unwelcome, call a professional, such as a shaman or spiritualist, who is trained in spiritual matters to help you handle the portal. Otherwise you may accidentally escalate your situation, and have it become much worse than when it first started. A professional will know how to mitigate these types of circumstances. In the meantime, you may ask a sacred guardian to watch over the room. If you do this, make sure whatever object you use to represent them is not placed immediately at the foot of the portal. This avoids the object placement being seen as an act of aggression, preventing the situation becoming worse.

Vortices

Vortices carry energy and the energy can only go in one direction. They are very catalytic and dynamic. Their function is to make sure that energy runs smoothly and to equalize pressure between this world and the spirit realms. A vortex in and of itself is neutral in its energy. Since vortices act as shunts, what you feel is what they carry in their wake. Their intensity depends on how much energy they have to shuttle to make things harmonious. Vortices cannot be changed but can be interacted with so that they can be beneficial for your household.

If a vortex is outward bound, it can be employed to help you remove obstacles or excess energy. You can place an object within the vortex's radius of influence that represents what you need help with. For example, let's say I am working on myself to reduce negative self-talk. I could put a journal on a table by the vortex in my space to assist me with letting go of toxic habits. I could also hang reminders on the wall of the bad habits that I'm trying to break.

As another example, let's say there is an excess of hyperactivity in my environment. I could place an object or an image that represents what that hyperactivity looks or feels like to me, along with what I want the end result to be. The vortex would draw into itself the excess energy of my space, leaving behind a more harmonious feeling.

If the vortex in your space is inward bound, it can help you bring in sacred energy, rejuvenation, and assist with manifestation. The procedure and cautions you would follow here would be identical to the steps for an inward bound portal.

Regardless of which way a vortex goes, it is important to be specific as to what it is that you want moved and the endpoint where you consider a space to be equalized. A vortex needs that gauge so that it can balance the energy so it ends up being useful, harmonious, and healthy.

⟡ EXERCISE ⟡
GRIDDING A SPACE

Let's revisit the topic of gridding and give you a technique for gridding of a space This idea was first mentioned in chapter 6. The gridding of a space further defines, secures, and generates steadfast Power in it. Gridding refines the energy and keeps it on track in places that are hyperactive or prone to chaos. This idea is very similar to using a balancing pole when walking on a tightrope. The gridding of a space helps to keep things stable in an environment where conditions are constantly changing and the unexpected is normal.

Examples of spaces that would need gridding might include a public location where activities and people radically change, such as a meeting room, conference center, or a convention center. The types of people that are attracted to these various venues bring in dramatically different types of emotions and energy. However, in this situation there is a desire to make the space inviting to everyone, regardless of who is using it.

If you are a counselor or are in the healing arts, I strongly encourage you to grid your office. The energy in your office can shift radically if you are dealing with people who are working their way through trauma, catastrophe, or a life-altering event. The release of energy from the highly emotionally charged situations of people that are working through their issues can be staggering. As I stated previously, whenever there is a strong emotional response it can and *will* create an energetic residue at a location. A grid would help to keep the undercurrent of what is happening there on track. It would also reduce excess emotional disturbance because it would continuously cleanse the energy of the room.

Another situation where a grid could be useful would be when a space is directly down a hallway or adjoining an area or property where there are toxic people, routine pandemonium, or counterproductive energy. In all these situations, the use of a grid will assist you in being able to comfortably coexist in your location, despite the unquenchable chaos that can be around you.

Although there are many configurations to grid a room, I am going to teach you the most basic one. To start, simply place an anchoring item in each corner of your space. These items need to be made of an earth element, like stone, and not a living being like a plant or wood. The reason for this is because these anchors will be in places of extreme turbulence; wood and living plants are too flexible and should only be used in environments with light or average energy. Putting a poor plant in the middle of an intense energetic cyclone would sentence it to death. The anchor has to be in proportion to the level of instability. If there is only minor chaos, then items made of wood could be sufficient. I still would not recommend a living plant. If you used a plant, in time you would find that it would grow to be either stunted or develop in a very odd way.

Grid points do not always *have* to be at the cardinal points, but they *do* need to be at the four extreme points within your space so that they can create a field of effect. However, it does matter if the corners of the room are close to the cardinal compass points or somewhere in the Walking Winds because that will determine the amount of Power you will need to create the consistent field that you desire.

Rooms with corners that fall in the directions of the Walking Winds positions can easily intensify chaotic energy. If you find your corners to fall in those directions, put an extra stone or crystal there to reinforce your intentions. The stones and crystals that you use do not need to be huge nor expensive nor fancy. They should however be in proportion or greater to the level of energy they are they are supposed to modulate. This includes fortifying healthy energy flow as well as keeping harmful energy at bay. There always needs to be a clear definition of what energy you wish to put into a space. What blessing or quality do you feel you need in order to make the space friendlier for you to spend time in it?

For example, a space intended for teaching can be a place of happy chaos and minor drama. This is a space where the people who gather are noisy as they enthusiastically learn how to create a crafting project or learn a new skill. Putting four small pebbles in each corner would not be sufficient for the tremendous uproar that ten or more young people and their guardians can create. In this case, a stone about the size of an orange could handle all the energy. I personally would use river or field stones, rose quartz, aventurine, or labradorite.

The way to judge the size of the stone needed is to feel the level of chaos that you are trying to calm. Feel and think about how much the energy needs to quiet down. The feeling is similar to trying to judge how loudly to speak when there is music playing or a group of people talking. The stone that you pick should be of the caliber and of the size to handle the intensity of the erratic energy that you are mitigating. This does not mean you need to bring four monoliths for each corner of the room if you are dealing with pandemonium! Instead, you can pick stones with qualities strong enough to handle these intense energies effectively. Examples might include obsidian, petrified wood, smoky quartz, or hematite.

How do you determine which stone or crystal to use? I would recommend that you refer to a good crystal book, such as *Love Is in the Earth* by author Melody, or the *Crystal Bible* by Judy Hall. There are also good sources online. As with anything, make sure that you look up more than one source of information. Most importantly, pay attention to how a stone makes you feel. This will give you a clue as to whether or not the stone will be the proper ally for what you need to do.

Before placing any stones or anchor items, it is imperative that you bless them, in addition to physically cleaning them. From a practical standpoint, the stones and crystals will look much more attractive as people look upon them. From a spiritual aspect, your physical contact with the items as you cleanse them connects you with their energy while you focus on what you are asking the stones to do. This is the respectful way to awaken them to their purpose.

To place your anchors inside your space, begin by facing the door and then start in the corner to the right of the door. Move clockwise to the other corners. Why does it matter where you begin, you may ask. The entrance of a space always ushers in new activity. When you move clockwise around the room it mimics how we perceive the movement of the sun across the sky. It is the way of order. The reason for starting closest to the door is because the door is where there is always an influx and exit of new energy. Because of this, it is key to anchor that energy point first as you grid and continue to concentrate on what it is you are asking the crystals to do. You are not done placing all the stones and crystals in the corners of the room until you finish your circle. In other words, walk back to the starting point so that you can form a *closed* grid of protection and blessings! After that, go to the center of the room, close your eyes, and focus on the stabilizing elements and energies that you want there.

Envision the four stones creating your desired field of Power that saturates the entire space from wall to wall, floor to ceiling. You can do this by envisioning a color. For example, say in this room of creative chaos I wish to bring an energy of happy focus. For me, that color is a blue green turquoise color. I would go to the center of the room and with my Heart focus on what the words peace and creativity mean to me and what they feel like. I would also envision the color turquoise, which holds the energy and embodiment of these words, permeating the entire room following the path from when I placed the circle of stones, back to the center and from there feeling this color saturating the entire room.

You could use more than four stones along the wall, but this can be highly impractical. You do not need people tripping or kicking stones and crystals around your room. You know you will have done the gridding right when the nervous or chaotic undercurrent feels comfortably under control. You will also notice that people will calm down in that room much more quickly and when they leave that it does not take that long for the room to reset itself after it filters out the extra, unnecessary energy.

Places of Honoring and Remembrance

While crafting your spaces, never forget to make space for places of honoring. These are places where we put pictures and tokens of our loved ones, both living and those that have crossed over. These places of honoring act as anchors of intention and a reinforcement of the quality of the energy and mood you want supporting your cause. Make sure that these areas of honor are placed as a focal point of the room they are in.

If the space for honoring is in a residence, then these mementos should be in a room where you want to deepen family bonds. If the place for honoring is in a public space, then the placement of the mementos should be in a spot intended to lift morale and give encouragement. In a work space, a space for honoring could include certificates, pictures of employees of the month, or plaques commemorating special achievements.

If you want energy from this area of remembrance to increase throughout an entire building, the area of remembrance should be placed in a corridor or stairwell where the Power is freely traveling throughout the building. This is similar to when you dip something in moving water. As the Power flows and moves, it begins to disperse what you have placed in its stream. Any energetic quality you wish to have permeate throughout your entire room or building needs to be placed in a corridor or stairwell.

Inviting a Divine Being into Your Home

Whether you're inviting a human or spiritual being to reside with you, it's important to be careful and think things through before you do this. Just as I have spent time talking to you about how to bring energetic elements into your space to create greater harmony and peace, I now will speak about bringing in a stronger spiritual element. In the tradition of the Good Red Road, there is always practicality and spirituality. I strongly encourage you to have a place to commemorate your spiritual helpers.

Just as you would have a nook or shelf to celebrate your relationship with an earthly loved one, there needs to be a place to honor the sacred spirits that you wish to invite into your home. The space does not need to be large. I live in a small home and I have dedicated one portion of my dresser to honor my patron, Lord Feathered Serpent. The honoring does not need to be limited to just one space. You could use different colors and symbols to honor a divine being throughout your home. This type of observance is a respectful request for beneficial blessings and flows of benign energy from that sacred spirit.

If there is no specific god, goddess, or sacred spirit that you are strongly called to, but you have a few in mind that you are considering inviting into your home, this is *the* time to research them! Even if you are familiar with the divine being you would like to solicit, go through the extra effort to learn what this one watches over and what is pleasing for this sacred being. This is no different from taking the time to learn what makes your loved ones happy and making sure they can feel at home. The research will also give you insights and information in case this divine entity spirit has requirements or restrictions that would affect your practices or lifestyle.

Just as with your loved ones, divine beings can vary greatly in what they prefer. If I wish to welcome the Wolf spirit into my home, I would have at least one place in my home where an image or some sort of representation of the Wolf itself resides. This sacred teacher watches over and reinforces the lessons of family and learning. With this knowledge, I would dedicate a space within my family room or my study to the spirit of the Wolf.

This would be very different if I were trying to honor the Archangel Michael. Yes, just like the others, I would have a place that either would hold an image of this archangel or a symbol of him. However, one of the things that pleases this archangel is acts of kindness, honor, and bravery. To honor Archangel Michael, I would have space in my home where I would offer hospitality and perform good deeds and acts of kindness outside my home.

Remember, any divine being you invite to reside in your home is another honored member of your family! You should not be afraid of punishment or be forced to live in a way that is unnatural to you. The exception would be if you chose a deity or spirit that has a stricter code of discipline or if you intentionally go against a restriction or requirement that is asked of you.

If you have done your research properly, you will know beforehand if this honored spiritual family member will be in perfect alignment with how you wish to live and what you believe in. You must also know ahead of time how you should approach these sacred spirits and if there are any special offerings that need to be made as you are making your request.

Once you are done your research, acquire any necessary effigies or specific symbols that would honor this divine spirit. When you place these items in your space, remember to bring energy from your Heart. The random placing of items means absolutely nothing if it's not done from the Heart. Unless a particular god or goddess has specific demands, the symbols and items can go anywhere in your room as long as they are not in a spot where they will be touched recklessly and without permission.

Although this step is optional, I strongly recommend that you do it. Even though you may already know the divine spirit that you wish to have reside with you, it is always better to connect with them before formally introducing them to your household. Just like you and I, they appreciate being invited rather than being shoved into a house or room. Make no mistake, however, this is not to say that we are equal to them! It is more along the lines of remembering your place. These are very powerful beings, much more powerful than us, and it is important to always approach them with reverence and respect. Think about it. You would definitely have more decorum and be mindful about how you welcome someone at your home if it were someone you admire or a leader of some sort. This should be the case when dealing with a god, goddess, or other blessed being.

⟫⟳ EXERCISE ⟳⟫
REQUESTING A DIVINE PRESENCE
IN YOUR SPACE

1. Before starting, make sure that you are prepared by having some items in mind and present to represent this divine being as you are performing this spiritual exercise. Make sure that you cannot be disturbed and that all electronic

devices are shut down. This exercise has no set time limit and can take anywhere from a few minutes to less than half an hour. Smudge yourself, the space you are doing this exercise in, and any items that you want considered by this divine entity.

2. Take time to pray, meditate, or journey. If there is particular ritual or routine that is requisite by this god, goddess, or sacred spirit, then perform that. If not, then it is okay to do your own practice. If you do not have a practice for meditation, journeying, or prayer, taking quiet time to contemplate and speak from your Heart is sufficient.

3. Reach out to the divine being with your Heart. Ask if they would like to be with you and if there is anything or any specific manner that they would like to be honored with.

4. When you are done, or if you are dismissed, give thanks for the time you were given to be heard. This ritual is now over.

5. Interpret what you have been given. If you feel a peace or warmth as you are doing the prayers and meditations, it means that the items you have presented are acceptable. At times you might get flashes of insight of adding something new a few days afterwards. This is normal. Requests from a divine being will always be compassionate and in relation to what you can reasonably do! It is possible to honor more than one sacred spirit. You need to follow this procedure each time with each one individually.

Just like any other relationship, you will get out of it what you put into it. The setting up of an honoring space and symbols but then forgetting about it will cause the blessings to fade over time or, even worse, feel the displeasure of the divine spirit. We all have been in those relationships where someone was a friend and they slowly drift away. We might still be open to them but we no longer feel close to them. Because of this, I would encourage you to create a meaningful routine of meditation prayer or contemplation. Every time you do this, you should honor the relationship that you have with the sacred being to keep it strong.

Say I wanted to honor the spirit of the east, who watches over new beginnings and new creations. I could set the symbol or the colors of the east to represent a sunrise in the room where I craft sacred items or where I do my writing. However, if I was honoring the Archangel Ariel, who watches over animals, I could put a symbol of the archangel where my animals and I tend to spend time together. Placing these symbols in an appropriate location shows respect and that I am paying attention to the unique preference of each of these beings. My continuing positive activities in alignment with what they watch over fortifies my bond with each of them.

Doing acts of devotion outside of your home will also reinforce your relationship with a holy being. It is very similar to going out and bringing home a thoughtful little gift or a favorite food or drink for a loved one to surprise them.

PROTECTIONS

All things in nature have a way of protecting themselves. Roses have thorns, porcupines have quills, and our own bodies have an immune system. It is unfortunate, but true, that not all things in our environment and in the spirit world are benign. Places subject to or in the vicinity of unrest, historic trauma, or malign energy would greatly benefit from creating a protective space within them.

After a physical and spiritual cleansing has been performed, installing a place of protection will establish the new energy where poisons of the past or present continue to be released. The toxic energy is channeled to ground in a protective space so that it is rendered harmless and avoids hurting others.

Making an area like this is not difficult, but it does require some forethought before putting it into action. Creating a place specifically for protection within a dwelling helps to boost the space's spiritual immune system and provides a wellspring of good, healthy energy. There are two basic types of spaces that you can create in order to have this effect.

The first type of space I actually already mentioned in the discussion on divine beings. Having a place of devotion to a divine being automatically introduces holy energy. The presence of this powerful being automatically creates a powerful field of protection and greatly increases the blessings of a building. This effect is even more pronounced when the divine being is renowned for protection against evil.

The second space is a place where you meditate and is dedicated to specific universal values, such as compassion. These are very potent locations that provide protection and centeredness. What I must emphasize for this type of protective spot is that you *must* connect heaven with earth! This will ground negative energy and render it neutral, much like a lightning rod redirects lightning to protect a building. This is accomplished by making sure you have some element of nature represented in a dynamic way, whether it be with plants, a water fountain, wind chimes, or a candle or incense.

Doing this helps to channel the energy from heaven to earth and back again, completing a Sacred Hoop. You are converting your space into a place where Waterfall energy, discussed in chapter 3, is constantly active.

Although not a form of protection per se, anything that bumps up good thoughts, good feelings, and good energy in a healthy way will vastly boost the energetic immune system of your space. This is similar to the concept of taking vitamin C to bolster your immune system. A positive environment that engenders optimism and good will generates positive energy and bolsters an ambience of constructive creativity.

Think about how you feel when you are in a location where you can be completely immersed in something that gives you joy or where you can work off your frustrations, and how it lifts your spirits and feeling of well-being in a huge way. I must caution you that even though this provides huge amounts of beneficial energy, it is not the same as a protection space designed specifically to ward off evil or malice that is directed personally at you.

It is an asset to have a protective space even if you are not in an area that is prone to toxic energy and negative chaos. Having a room or even a small space that is dedicated to combating the negativity you might face on a regular basis assists in turning poison into sweet water. Minimizing your exposure to toxins, both physically and energetically, boosts your health and improves your overall quality of life.

A protective space also provides a stable place of positive Power where like attracts like. This positive energy can rejuvenate you, in addition to giving you the opportunity to think clearly and reconnect with your body and your spirit. Having a protective space is a gift of solace and safety for yourself and those who are with you. A protective space helps to repel weaker toxic beings, such as bad chaos spirits. Bad chaos spirits are entities that are attracted to toxic emotions and patterns. They feed off of pain, misery, and depression. A home or work space that is full of serenity and optimism is very repellent and poisonous to these beings. It will also help to lessen the chance of mischievous and transient spirits coming to your space.

When there is discord or unnecessary chaos, it acts like a homing beacon to beings that thrive on mischief. Mischievous spirits bring confusion and tension and some can act like angry poltergeists. Transient spirits can bring a sense of unrest or depression, in addition to whatever memories and other energies that touched them before they crossed over. Having a strong protective field will help to repel negative energy and make space for that which is life-sustaining and nourishing.

Dealing with Unwanted Spirits

It is not uncommon to have an odd transient spirit being passing through. Do not hold on to the idea about making threats to kick the spirit out. However, before you claim that there is spiritual activity, try your best to debunk it first! Pay attention to see if there are any quirks that your space might have, such as an old drafty window that produces cold spots or a house that is settling and making weird noises. A buggy electric system can cause odd light phenomena. I have been out with several paranormal investigation units, and many times there was absolutely no supernatural activity but a previously unknown house repair that needed to be completed.

I would like to give you two cautionary tales to consider if you should have, or think you have, an unexpected unseen guest in your home or work place. I remember years ago helping a family in New York. They purchased a very lovely older home through an estate auction. The young couple delightedly moved in with their new baby. They grew increasingly alarmed as they kept on seeing the ghost of an elderly woman appearing by their infant daughter's crib throughout the day and night. The ghost of the elderly woman never caused them any harm, and the little one would smile and coo at the ghost. However, the idea of this unknown entity near their baby daughter made them extremely apprehensive. Another daily phenomena was that every time they shut the door to the upstairs family room, it would open back up. This would happen even if they locked the door.

The couple had heard that they could get rid of ghosts by performing a very thorough smudging, along with a very strong, harsh, and heartfelt demand that she leave. When they did this, they felt a wave of sadness, but after that it was quiet. The young parents were happy thinking that they had succeeded, but their peace did not last long. After about a month, there came another entity, the ghost of a large man. This ghost was darker and brought with it feelings of dread and anger. They would experience poltergeist-like activities, which deeply frightened the new family. The ghost was especially aggressive to the mother and it was not uncommon for the baby to shriek in complete horror. They tried twice to perform the same ritual as they did with the spirit of the old woman. The result was retaliation from the ghost with more frequent terrifying hauntings and physical attacks.

Around that time, I was called in to help. I performed the necessary ceremonies and was successful in removing the malicious entity. I had them research the history of the house. Through their research, they learned there had been an older lady, a widow, who lived there by herself for many years. She was very kind, loved by the neighbors, and enjoyed watching over her grandchildren.

However, previous to the widow, there had been a family that had an abusive man who beat and abused his wife and children. When the young couple had commanded the spirit of the elderly woman to leave, it left an energetic vacuum that created an opening for the angry spirit to move in. In addition, it is not uncommon for a young child or an infant to attract spiritual activity. This is because the life force of little ones is very strong because they are still so close to the spirit world.

Interestingly enough, the spirit of the older woman reached out to me after I had removed the angry man's spirit. All she wanted was to have permission to visit the home she cherished so much in life. She requested that the door to the upstairs sitting room be kept open so she could sit and watch out the window, gazing at the neighborhood she loved so well. She also asked if she could visit them and their baby girl because it reminded her of her own family. She promised never to frighten them.

At first the couple was not thrilled, but they soon came to love her and call her nanny. This spirit became an extra set of eyes for the young mother because she would make the mother aware whenever her daughter needed anything. As time went by, the elderly woman's ghost would help the little girl to be unafraid at night by being a protective spirit.

Although the idea might seem strange, at times it is not the spiritual entity who is the invader, we are! I remember another case I was called to in Virginia many years back. In this case, the home was newly constructed on the top of a small wooded mountain. Since the owner was an architect, he designed his house to perfectly match the needs of his growing family. He wanted it to be the home that he and his wife would grow old in, have their children in, and, in time, grandchildren.

However, from the very beginning, construction of the building seemed jinxed. Odd things began to happen and only increased in intensity after the family moved in. Some of the phenomena they experienced included objects moving on their own, a dark fleeting shadow darting periodically throughout the house, and a sense of threatening dread. No one was ever harmed, and oddly enough, the two dogs of the family would happily wag their tails and eagerly bark as if greeting an old friend before the disturbances would begin.

Full of fear and thinking they were doing the right thing, this family also attempted an ill-conceived exorcism using smudge and forceful language. The haunting became much more intense after the attempted exorcism. The family would hear ghostly footfalls and a dark figure about the size of a man would be seen walking through the place. Objects were thrown across rooms and smashed. Things requiring expensive repairs, such as the plumbing, would inexplicably break down. At times, they heard what sounded like drums or the voice of an angry man, but the words could not be made out. The overall sense of not being welcome in their own home grew to such a point that the family would stay away from the house as much as possible. Any repairs that were started would be thwarted and freak accidents would happen. The accidents were always enough to seriously stall any work, but never to injure anyone.

Soon after, I was called in to help. Upon doing my prayers, I was allowed to shamanically connect with the entity. I learned that this being was not evil at all but rather a very angry and outraged Sacred Ancestor of the Land. From the spirit's point of view, imagine being happy in your own home, minding your own business. Suddenly, some intruders come in and completely destroy your house and the land around you. These interlopers have the nerve to settle in, and, to make matters even worse, once you begin to complain and try to kick them out, these unin-vited guests attempt to throw *you* out of your own home with the very same rituals of your own people! I do not know about you, but that would seriously infuriate me. I explained this to the family. The owner confirmed that the land his house was sitting on and the surrounding area was historically known to be a location where the local Native American tribes used to live and hold sacred ceremonies to honor the Creator and the land. This entity was an outraged Sacred Ancestor of Land, one of the many benign spirit beings of that area who had watched over and blessed the tribes that used to live there.

Upon learning this, I relayed the information to the very skeptical family. Although they were very unsure about what I shared, they were desperate and took my advice. The family needed to make amends with this divine being. Only after seeking forgiveness might they ask permission to dwell there.

When I journeyed, I learned that the Sacred Ancestor of the Land required a native tree species to be grown to honor the spirits and the indigenous people who had dwelt there before them. The tree needed to be kept well so it could provide nourishment, physically and spiritually, for humans, spirits, and animals alike. The land and surrounding woods were to be cherished and preserved. Fortunately, the family did as was requested of them and more.

Since they liked apples, they planted an apple tree. For good measure, I taught them a simple honoring ceremony when it was time to harvest the apples. They also planted a small grove of eastern redbud trees. As the years went by, the trees grew more beautiful, and as they matured the family prospered too. What about the Sacred Ancestor of the Land? The blessed spirit adopted the family and became their protector and guardian.

The lesson of these examples is that what is easy to escalate is not so easy to diffuse! I would like to take away some of the mystery and introduce some common sense when it comes to this topic. Let us pretend that we're working not with some unseen entity, but a human being. Under normal circumstances, your first inclination would not be to pick a fight. If there was tension, I am very sure you would do your level best not to instigate any further hostility. You would try to see where the misunderstanding and miscommunication came from with this individual and then see where to go from there. So, just as you would with an unknown person, do the same thing with a spirit. If a situation felt threatening with a person, you would call the police immediately. If you feel that an entity is intimidating, then you should call on someone who is specifically trained to handle these situations, such as your friendly neighborhood shaman or other expert spiritual practitioner.

In my experience, the majority of the paranormal cases involve spirits that act like a normal stranger who is levelheaded and means you no harm. An offering of goodwill, such as respectfully talking through a misunderstanding so that a reasonable and friendly resolution can be reached, is the proper course of action.

In the case of an unknown spirit, never offer a place to stay in your home until you know more about them! It is the same precaution that you would take before offering a random stranger a place to stay in your home. As with any misunderstanding, you would explain that you mean no offense to them, but that you will not tolerate being treated in a manner that frightens or potentially harms you, your family members, or your animal companions in any way. Have the same attitude with an unseen guest as you would with someone who accidentally walked into your house or a private event. You would firmly, but politely, ask them to kindly leave in peace. The average person, or spirit, who made the mistake would apologize and be grateful that there was an easy conclusion of this awkward situation and that both parties saved face.

However, if things get worse or feel worse, you would call in a professional! If you had someone who is of ill intent, or not in their right mind or senses, and becomes increasingly hostile no matter what you do, you would call the authorities. The same rule applies here. If you have an unseen entity that is becoming more and more threatening, call in an expert who knows how to handle this type of situation.

In my personal opinion, it is not a bad idea to have someone who has a good reputation and is well trained in talking to the spirits, and other nature entities such as elementals or earth spirits, to come over anyway. It does not do any harm to have a second opinion to give you fresh insights or validate what you have been sensing. Just as you would for any other service, it is important to check the ethics and background of the practitioner! Only a con artist would casually say that you are cursed, frighten you, and then make more and more demands of you, costing several hundreds or thousands of dollars to liberate you. The primary focus of any ethical spiritual practitioner will always be the welfare of all involved, seen *and* unseen! They will do their very best to guide the situation to the best possible conclusion. If they charge, it should be a fair price with a detailed explanation of what you can realistically expect. Think of the type of questions you would ask of any expert in any other field, such as a surgeon or a major home remodeler, before you contract them. These are the same types of questions you would ask before hiring an expert spiritual practitioner.

Eight
MAINTAINING YOUR SPACE

ᕙᕗ

YOU HAVE DONE VERY WELL to come this far! After all this hard work, it is important to be able to maintain the wanted energies of your spaces, and with a few simple habits, I promise you it will not be that hard. It is paramount to set up a series of routines.

One of the big ones is to make it a habit to cull clutter! I have been guilty of working very hard to clear space only to have it fill back up time and again with unnecessary or misplaced items. Make it a routine to avoid buying unnecessary items or follow the idea that when something new comes in, something old *must* come out. It helps to cut down on the amassing of things that fill your place and make it crowded. For some people it might be difficult to get rid of anything old, for various reasons. However, you need to move beyond the thought of "But I might need it later!" If you are not sure you want to get rid of an item, put a date on it and put it away. Give a deadline of one to a *maximum* of three months and see how frequently you used it, if at all. If you have not used it by that third month, let it go!

The same can be said about collections. Unless properly displayed, collections can begin to look like a garage sale. It is better to put some pieces out on display so they can be appreciated, and then rotate them throughout the year. That way each of your pieces can be given the spotlight and appreciated. When you put one item away and put out another item from your collection, it will seem new again because you have not seen it for a while. I always recommend, if at all possible, to display any collection in such a way that it is easy to maintain and dusting will be kept at a minimum, such as using a shadowbox or cabinet with glass windows.

So how do you know when there are too many items on display? That is very simple! Try the "ugh test." This test describes the feeling when you have to do housekeeping and you look around, let out a great sigh and then say "Ugh! This is just going to be too much bother; I will just do this tomorrow." Of course, tomorrow never comes and the dust bunnies grow bigger and more abundant until you repeat this process.

Let's face it, it's rare to find someone who enjoys housekeeping. Your place is supposed to keep you and yours happy, not become a burden. Better yet, do not let yourself get anywhere near that saturation point. Decide how much time you want to spend with housekeeping, find or make some earth friendly cleaning products, and then learn the most efficient way to do your chores. This is why, if you have ever been away, you will notice that hotel rooms, bed-and-breakfasts, or other places with tourists keep decorations at a minimum. The decoration is kept minimum not just because they want to keep things appealing to many tastes, but because cleaning crews need to be thorough and efficient to welcome the next set of guests as quickly as possible. Once you find your routines, you will see that this is much easier.

I cannot stress enough how much I like multifunctional items, and especially functional art! Items that perform more than one function not only will save you space, they will also save you time. I personally like functional art, such as decorated throw pillows or handmade pottery. They serve a dual function of beautifying my space and, because it is something that I use on a daily basis, I get to enjoy it every day and justify its existence in my home.

If you find yourself developing a clutter habit, or becoming a pack rat, pay attention to what might be causing you unrest. Clutter can be very much like stress eating! Sometimes when we are unhappy with ourselves, there will be a tendency to collect items by either impulse buying or becoming lazy about putting them away. Clutter can also be a response to trying to fill an empty place within yourself instead of something nourishing that has substance, such as getting counseling or making new friendships.

It is vital to keep things organized, rather than just neat. You can have a space that is neat as a pin but completely impractical. It can be extremely frustrating when something looks as perfect as a movie set, but everything you need requires an extra step to be able to get it or to put it away. In short time, you will find yourself falling into chaos because your place is arranged in a way that is not harmonious with your reasoning of where things should go. If something is organized, it will look tidy *and* have frequently used items easily accessible. Items that you use on a daily basis should be kept where you can have them on hand always. Other items that are seasonal or are rarely used can be stored in harder to reach places. There is no one right way to do this!

Yes, it is true that there are basic tips on how to keep things neat so that they are also organized, but only you can say what should take a prime position within a cabinet, drawer, or shelf. There is something to be said about proper storage. I recommend you keep yourself updated on how you organize your things so they can remain neat depending on your changing needs. Making sure that you have storage bins or other containers to keep things handy and easily put away is key. It will save you so much time when you need something and you know exactly where it is.

This also applies to thinking ahead before you start collecting and displaying your treasures. Label things and make a list of every item as you put it away so that you know what is in a certain box or basket. Label boxes on more than one side. Trust me, it will help you save a *ton* of time! The few extra seconds you take in patiently making a label will prevent a huge amount of frustration and delay when you no longer remember what you have placed in a particular container.

Remember that your space is an extension of you, and, in turn, both you and your place are extensions of our beautiful Earth Mother. The reason I mention this is because you will find that your space will have its own form of moods. These moods will become very palpable when you walk into a space and can feel how the ambience has changed.

One way to keep your place in balance is to keep it in sync with the seasons. From a practical standpoint, adjusting to these changes, such as using more natural lighting when it is a bright day or closing windows on a cold night, will save you energy. Also, decorating your place in relation to the seasons can help to bring the outside in and reinforce the connection of your space as being part of the greater planet. Pay attention to anything that has gone on in your space has been tense, anxiety-filled, or depressed. Take steps to clear and clean your area not only physically but energetically. If you do this, you will find that the ambience will always feel fresh and full of life. It is much nicer to walk into a space that is inviting and feels open and ready to receive you versus one that feels stressful from the activities or disputes that might have gone on in it.

The only constant is change! We are always evolving and changing, therefore it is important to make sure that your place is kept current. The areas that you and those who reside with you spend the most time in should reflect the changes of mood and interest as all of you change over time. This is especially true during times of transition where there can be profound internal shifting that affects lifestyle, traditions, and routines.

What I find interesting is that people will naturally change their homes for the coming of a baby or the addition of a new animal companion, but for some reason they are reluctant to do this when it comes to turning a page in their own lives. It is okay. We all do this and it is normal. The reason being is that there is the thought, conscious or subconscious, that if you let things go or update them, you will lose the echo of memory of a special loved one or of your children when they were happily running throughout your house. Yes, you are right, but I would like to remind you of a greater truth.

What you value **never** *leaves you!* Just like you, your home or work space is meant to evolve and change expression to reflect where you are now. Think back on what used to give you joy and security as a child. Now, imagine yourself doing those activities *exactly* like that today. I can feel your grin from here. It would seem absurd! And, of course, you are right. I value friendship. When I was younger and several of us were not yet married nor had children, it was easy enough to go out, or have people come over and stay until late into the evening. As the years passed and my children came into the picture, that was no longer the case. Fast-forward several more years and now they are grown and starting their own adult lives. I have let go of my bigger home and table because all that they would be doing is taking up space. Doing so has given back to me a huge amount of time and allowed for me to write my books and enjoy spending time with you, dear reader. I have since changed up those large furniture pieces for some smaller, cozier items and smaller tables, which aid in having pleasant conversations in a warm, intimate setting. I still value friendship and always will, but its expression has evolved between my friends and I. Going with the flow of change as the years have winged by has allowed for our friendships to become stronger and not stilted by trying to hold on to a past that has long since ceased to be.

RESETTING ENERGY AFTER A MAJOR LOSS OR TRANSITION

On the Good Red Road, things are not seen in a straight line, but rather as a Sacred Hoop. Events come and go, expressing themselves a little bit differently every time. These changes don't necessarily follow just the death of a loved one, but it could be the ending of a stage of life for you. The most common are becoming an empty nester, retirement, or a sudden change in life that feels traumatic or unsettling. Regardless of the triggering event, it is important to have compassion for yourself and others.

In order to avoid creating stagnant energy, or, even worse, a place that seems like it sucks the life force out of everything and everyone, it is mandatory to let go of the old energy in order for it to move on.

Life is an ever-flowing cycle of new beginnings growing into new ways of being, letting go, and death in order to be able to make space for new life and energy to begin the process all over again. Death and loss are as much of a part of life as is birth and growth. In several Native American traditions, after someone crosses over there is a releasing ceremony. Within the first moon or month from when their bodies die, there is typically a form of a giveaway ritual. As is the custom on the Good Red Road, everything has to be both spiritual and practical in order for it to be useful.

When you give away a deceased person's possessions, what you are doing from an energetic and spiritual standpoint is releasing the earthly hold upon their spirits so they may journey in peace. From a physical and practical viewpoint, these items can go on to help others and, if appropriate, act as mementos. This is not to say that you are not allowed to keep precious items! Significant keepsakes serve an important function of holding close to us the loving energy and memories of that very special person or animal that we miss so much. Allowing time for proper grieving and processing the sorrow will ease the transition, both physically and in your heart, to be receptive for new life.

It is a very normal reaction to want to hold on to these items as long as you can because, in a way, it is like being able to hold on to the one you love, but it is not healthy. Since grief is a very personal thing, you must allow yourself the time you need and go through the natural process of it. It is okay to have a place of remembrance so long as it does not prevent you from moving forward, a spot where there are photographs that bring you happy memories of your loved ones and perhaps a few sentimental items that you hold dear. As for the rest of the possessions that belonged to that individual, it is not really the physical items that you want to hold on to. I recommend taking a picture of the items and then writing the memory and feeling that these things represent. Donate what is usable to another person so it can enrich their lives and know that the energy and blessing will move onto them.

However, it can also be that the person whom you are releasing may have had some toxic energy attached to them and this nasty residue clings to their possessions. In this particular case, cleanse the items before you donate them. That way the person who receives these objects will be able to make good use of them without bringing in unwanted energy unknowingly.

Getting Rid of Clutter

Compare what you have in relation to how well it matches your future purposes. In order to determine what stays and what goes, follow some simple guidelines. How easy is it to maintain? Is the item truly something that you will use? Does the item in question not only serve its function but help to support the overall feeling and energy that you are trying to create? Sometimes it can be very difficult to decide whether you should keep an item or not. This is how we end up accumulating things. More often than not, an item is kept because it keeps the feeling of a memory alive. The phrase "But I might need it someday" is the bane of being able to live simply.

Use my suggestion from earlier about putting items into a box and seeing if you use them in a three-month time span. If you have not opened the box by that point, then you do not need that item! I know for many people clothing items can be the bigger issue. I follow a similar strategy here. At the beginning of a season I hang all of the hangers in the opposite direction from what I regularly would. When I use an item of clothing I put the hanger back in the way that it would normally go. By the end of a season, I can instantly see which articles of clothing I consistently used and which I did not.

If you do not usually hang your clothes but instead put them into drawers, when you fold your clothing, put it upside down or facing the opposite direction in the drawer than you normally would. I like wearing heavier sweaters during the winter. Sometimes I am not too sure if the sweaters still suit my style but I really want to keep them. I fold them up carefully and put them with the neck facing the bottom of the drawer, which is the opposite way that I normally would store it. The same rules apply here: anything that remains upside down or facing the opposite direction needs to be given away.

If you have a hard time figuring out where to begin, then remove the biggest items first. You will find that if you move the biggest items first it begins to create a positive domino effect. Of course, moving that big object forces you to look at other smaller possessions that are on the shelf or are cluttered on top of or around a piece of furniture. Focus on one thing at a time! Although it might be tempting to want to tackle the whole room at once, tackling the biggest item first and thoroughly resolving it will help to build excitement and momentum for continuing on with the smaller things.

This habit of streamlining is not only limited to possessions. Remember that you are trying to create a space that will support you and those who are with you now, in addition to the different events that will be held at your place in the future. It is necessary to take time to see how old ways of thinking and old habits have allowed things to become stagnant and impractical. This can be as simple as finding new ways of doing your housekeeping chores that save you time, or eliminating things that are contradictory to the function of a room, like removing idle pastimes if you are trying to design an office that is meant for productivity.

Routine Spiritual and Practical Housekeeping

I am now going to tackle a subject that nobody likes: housekeeping. The maxim that things *must* be both practical and spiritual also applies to housekeeping being done on a regular basis in order for your place to remain vibrant and alive. I want you to imagine, for a moment, that you washed your body only as often as you have done spiritual and energetic cleaning of your place. Are you grossed out yet? If so, then you understand that you need to perform regular hygiene of your home or work place not only physically but energetically as well. This will keep your place optimal and you will be happy with a place that is clean in spirit, body, and mind.

As said before, your home and work spaces are extensions of your body and, in turn, you and your place are directly connected to and are an extension of Earth Mother, both physically and spiritually. I will give you a few simple things to do so that it will be easy to keep up with housekeeping as you go along. Usually, maintaining your space is a simple affair, except if something dramatic or traumatic has happened. At that point a deeper cleansing might be necessary in order to reset your place.

I personally follow a regimen of monthly maintenance. You will find that once you have your routine set you will move through it very quickly and that it is no trouble at all. The reason why I advise doing it this frequently is because you can catch changes sooner instead of later if the energy starts going out of alignment. It is much easier to correct the energy if it is caught early versus when the misalignment grows in magnitude as time goes on. I liken this very much to routinely looking at and checking the food in your cupboard or in your refrigerator to make sure that you do not have any biology experiments growing in there. Getting rid of things that no longer serve you is much like throwing out food that has gone bad. It makes space for that which is nutritious and healthy.

໑⬥໑ EXERCISE ໑⬥໑
SPIRITUAL HOUSEKEEPING

Begin spiritually cleansing your space by going to the Heart of it and offering smudge to the Seven Arrows. You will only have to do this once in the beginning for the entire process. Connect with the Heart of your space by sitting there and reflecting on what the essence of the space is about. While putting your hands upon the item that represents the Heart of your space, feel within your own Heart the purpose of why you have created this place. Feel the emotional energy building up within you and then transfer that energy into the item that holds the Heart energy. Repeating this process with any significant possession fuels it. Do not forget to do the same procedure if you have honoring spaces to divine beings, Ancestors, and/or grids.

When you do this for your Ancestors, reflect on each one of them in turn and thank them for blessing and protecting your home. For a grid, focus while you are in the center of the room and when you are ready to release the Power you have built up inside your Heart, touch each of the stones and crystals briefly. When recharging your grid, touch the stones in the same order that you set them up in. If the space you're cleansing is a work space that houses reminders of your achievements, take time to look upon the items and remember the joy and pride of receiving these awards and certificates. Gently touching them while exhaling will release energy from within you and revitalize your connection.

If your space is established for honoring a divine being, a spiritual cleanse really should be done more frequently than once a month. However, this does depend on the god or goddess in question and how frequently they require your devotion. Take time to sit in respectful meditation and prayer, open your own heart, and allow yourself to receive messages from divine beings. While you are contemplating if you are moved, speak words of gratitude for the blessings you have received and are yet to receive.

If there are offerings or certain meditations or prayers that need to be done, do them at this time. I find that it is very effective to go with smudge throughout my entire place, cleaning the flow of energy through the corridors and in the rooms. Remember that you do not have to use smoke. If needed, you can make or purchase a spray made of essential oils or a light infusion of herbs. I make my own disinfecting all-purpose cleaner. I like putting in a small drop or two of essential oils, such as lavender or a combination of sage, cedar, and sweetgrass, so that whenever I am polishing or wiping down the items in my house I am also cleansing them spiritually.

I will share with you the recipe for the all-purpose cleaner that is environmentally friendly. It was given to me many years ago by my son's pediatrician because he was born prematurely. His lungs were very delicate and anything harsh, such as cleaning chemicals, would have made him seriously ill or even killed him. This all-purpose cleaner is pet friendly, in addition to being welcoming for sacred spirits. You may change the essence of the oil if you prefer a different scent. The idea is that not only is the cleaner pleasing to you, but it also has spiritual properties that help you to revitalize your space as you are doing your chores.

ᶜᐧ⌖ Exercise ⌖ᐧᶜ
All-Purpose Cleaner Recipe (One Gallon)

This recipe comes from a book called *Clean & Green: The Complete Guide to Nontoxic and Environmentally Safe Housekeeping* by Annie Berthold-Bond. I have increased the proportions because I use this so much in my home.[9]

Pour the following ingredients into a one gallon container:

- Two tablespoons plus two teaspoons of borax
- One tablespoon plus a teaspoon of washing soda
- One cup of vinegar
- One tablespoon and a teaspoon of a vegetable-based soap, such as castile soap. I personally like to use Dr. Bronner's with the essence of lavender because I can spiritually clean my home with the lavender the same time I am physically cleaning it. You can also use an unscented vegetable soap and add a few drops of essential oils or herbal infusions. Do not add too much or else you will leave an oily film or stain your items or counters when using this cleaner. If vitamin E or vitamin C (ascorbic acid) is not listed in the ingredients of your vegetable soap, you need to add a couple of drops of either one (usually found at your local health food store) per half gallon of liquid soap when you

---

9. Annie Berthold-Bond, *Clean & Green: The Complete Guide to Nontoxic and Environmentally Safe Housekeeping* (Woodstock, NY: Ceres Press, 1994), 25.

open the bottle for the first time to protect against possible nitrosamine contamination.[10]

Combine all of these ingredients with hot water to fill the gallon container. Shake until everything is *completely* dissolved. Pour the solution into any spray bottle you use to clean your space.

The solution will keep for up to three months, but must be stored in a cool, dark place. This has been a very good cleaner and has kept my spaces spotless through the years. You will find that making your own cleaners is not only friendly to our Earth Mother, but that you will feel good, in addition to saving a lot of money. I also play music while cleaning and find that it makes me happy while doing chores. Music can be used on a daily basis to reset and realign energy. Music is a very powerful and universal tool. The end result will be a place that you are very content to be in and others that come to visit you or stay with you will also feel the difference.

ANNUAL GRAND HOUSEKEEPING

Even though, ideally, you would do your physical and spiritual housekeeping on a weekly or monthly basis, it is still important to do at least one major cleansing annually. You could do it on a significant date, such as the start of the new year or the anniversary of when you acquired your space. Taking time to assess what is going on throughout the entire year will give you clear insight

---

10. Anne Minard, "Shampoo, Cosmetics May Form Cancer-Causing Substance in Water Supplies," *National Geographic*, May 1, 2010, https://www.nationalgeographic.com/news/2010/5/100429-shampoo-cancer-causing-substance/#close.

to decide if your place needs to be gently realigned, mildly reinforced, or if it needs to be entirely rebooted.

Imagine that you have just been through a rough year. For the year to come, you might wish to feed the Heart of your space with extra energy for healing. Or perhaps you have major life changes coming, such as a new child, or the expansion of a business venture. Infusing your place with energy that attracts abundance and asking your spiritual helpers to guide you with managing prosperity is a very wise course of action.

Give thanks for what you have been given throughout the year. In order to reinstate the current energy or to fine-tune it for what is coming, create an activity that embodies your intentions for the coming year. It could be as simple as you doing an activity that represents healing or prosperity. The more people that participate in the activity and share the same intention, especially by those who live or work in the same space, the greater the Power that is generated to sustain all of you for the rest of the year. There does not need to be a set time for the duration of this activity, but do not rush it! Taking time to show gratitude, mindfulness, and respect is a fundamental principle of the Heart of the Earth technique, which is both a spiritual and practical method. Just as you are performing this event charged with spiritual intention, so it must be followed through with the practical.

Do a walk-through of your place and assess if you need to get rid of anything old or if there is a need to bring in anything new. See if there have been any shifts of energy and where there may need to be some realignments. What is key during your annual grand housekeeping is to have a personal celebration that helps to revitalize and realign the Heart of your space. If you have any places that honor Ancestors or divine beings, there should be a spiritual rededication in each of these places and a reinforcing of the invitation.

Don't forget to reestablish the connection in honoring the natural world as you do this major cleansing and rededication. Just as you are strengthening the bonds of love and trust with your loved ones, seen and unseen, do not forget your wild relatives and the beings of nature. Creating this reestablished connection could be as simple as feeding the birds or supporting a charity that helps protect the environment and animals. You will be surprised at how good you will feel as their appreciation of your thoughtfulness is returned to you with many blessings being showered upon you and yours through the coming year.

Doing this annual grand housekeeping will be worth the trouble because as you do this, not only are you showing love and respect for those who support you, you are also performing some much-needed self-care. Make a habit of rewarding yourself every day by giving yourself a wonderful place to return to and to be in. Very few things in this world can be as comforting at the end of a long day as knowing you have a safe place to return to.

⊱ Exercise ⊰
Heart Renewing Ceremony

I would like to share with you a ceremony that could act as an example or springboard of one that you can create for yourself to use during your annual grand housekeeping. You will need:

- Smudge (using a smoke free version is fine)
- Paper and pen
- Candle or kindling of natural wood, grasses, plus some smudge if lighting a fire
- Matches or a lighter

- A way to extinguish fire if you light one
- Natural pipe tobacco if not using fire
- Any items you would like to add to strengthen the Heart of your space, sanctuary room, honoring places, or sacred spaces devoted to divine beings
- Any items for your celebration depending on what you have planned, such as food and nonalcoholic drinks
- (Optional) Gentle music, such as Native American flute music or meditative drumming

You need to know what the focus of your intentions will be to determine what items you will need ahead of time. In many Native American traditions, ceremonies start with prayers of gratitude and end with prayers of gratitude. In between the prayers of thanks, a strong Heart renewing ceremony would have three phases: release, renew, realign. Begin by smudging yourself, anyone else in attendance if you have invited others to participate, and all items. Offer the smudge to the Seven Arrows.

Release

One cannot fill a cup that is already full. You must release something before being able to receive. Think about what it is that you need to let go of in order to make space for the new. Doing a detailed cleaning of your home or work space and getting rid of all those white elephants is a wonderful way to kick off an annual releasing. I promise you it is worth the effort because you will have instant gratification and your place will begin to feel lighter and the energy will flow smoother.

Ritualistically, in order to let go of old energies or things that cause sorrow or chaos, there are two simple ceremonies that I would offer you. The first one is to light a fire in a safe place using some smudge. It does not have to be a big fire. It can be the size of a candle or it can be the size of a small bonfire, it is up to you. As always, safety first and follow all precautions in regards to handling a live flame, regardless of size. Take as many pieces of paper as you need to write down all the things that are toxic for you and that you wish to release. They can be personal things, but *never* write anything with the intention to harm or interfere with the welfare of another! Hold the piece of paper in your hand and put that hand against your heart. Release into that paper all those things which are negative and heavy. When you are ready, toss the paper into the fire. Please know that this is a sacred fire of purification and nothing else is to be allowed to be cast into it! It is permissible to snuff out the fire or pour water on it to douse it. You do not have to wait for the fire to completely burn out.

The second option, if fire is not practical or safe for you, is a similar ritual performed with natural pipe tobacco. As you did with the paper, take a pinch of tobacco and hold it in your hand and place that hand upon your heart. Just as you did with the paper, release into it all the things that you want to be free of for the coming year. Then, release the tobacco into the wind.

If you have done this properly, you will feel lighter and spiritually more clean, and have a sense of relief knowing that what you have asked to be taken from you by the Great Spirit is now leaving you to make space for that which is good and wonderful for the coming year.

Renew

In this portion of the ceremony, you would do things that affirm the values you live by, the blessings you are requesting, and strengthen the bonds of your helpers, seen and unseen. The idea is to show appreciation by celebrating those who have been with you and will continue to be by your side as you move forward.

This ritual is one of sharing favorite memories of the past season or year. If you are sharing this ritual with others, it should have a feeling of happiness, merriment, and community. If you are by yourself, the ritual should have a feeling of warmth and comfort, much like snuggling into blankets to enjoy a good rest after a long day. The ritual can also include enjoying some favorite foods and drinks. In many Native American traditions, before the community eats or drinks, a small plate is set aside with a taste of all the different foods that are being shared at the celebration. This plate is then placed outside and a splash of drink given to the Earth. This is known as a spirit plate. The idea is to give back gratitude and acknowledge all the blessings that you have been given.

When you are finished with this portion of the celebration, you should feel refreshed and clear as to your purpose and reason for living in your home or staying at your work place. It should be uplifting and meaningful.

Realign

At times, because the events of the previous season or year have knocked you off course or because what you achieved so far is not quite in alignment with where you are going, there is a need for realignment. This realignment will bring in new energies that must be introduced for the coming season or year to get everything back on track. The idea here is to do an activity that is an expression of the energy that you are trying to bring in.

The activity could be a simple ceremony of introducing an item that is symbolic of a quality or the energy that you are bringing in. If you're sharing the ceremony with others, gifting new things to each other could also be an activity to bring new energy in. Some examples of things you could introduce for new energy might include a water fountain to honor the element of water, planting a tree to honor the element of earth, or doing acts of kindness or charity to honor the element of spirit.

At the end of the Heart Renewing Ceremony, remember to complete the Sacred Hoop by giving thanks and do a closing thought and prayer. Just as your physical loved ones like being asked to come and thanked before they leave, the same thing applies to our allies in the spirit realms.

ADDITIONAL THOUGHTS TO CONSIDER FOR YOUR HEART RENEWAL CEREMONY

What you need for your Heart Renewal Ceremony depends on what you have planned. Having a simple and intimate gathering where everyone shares memories over food and drink would require a lot less planning and energy than if you are planning a party for a larger number of people. Another idea for a gathering activity that many people are drawn to is a drumming circle. Of course, this too would require a little bit of forethought and planning, including finding a place that enjoys the sound of drums, and possibly of people singing or chanting.

Although optional, I strongly counsel you to check with a good spiritual source as to what type of energy the year or season will bring. I am trained to interpret sacred time and the energy it will bring, which is also known as the Flow of the River. Weekly and annually, I share with my community and any who will listen what to anticipate and how to move harmoniously with the Flow of the River. I perform ceremonies to honor the turning of each of the four seasons and do prayers and meditations to learn what messages the divine spirits have for us. Spiritual connection gives you insight as to what types of energies and elements need to be introduced to stay in balance with Earth Mother and what to watch out for.

As a personal practice, I also pay attention to current affairs because I can then adjust my prayers and lifestyle changes to help the greater good. For example, one year I was working on bringing in creativity and prosperity, but I also kept hearing about companies that had bad practices that destroyed the rainforests and kept communities in poverty. Spiritually, I sent healing energy to the forests and all who dwell in them and to the communities seeking justice. I introduced more representations of the element of water, such as tiny fountains and sea shells, to my daily practices because one of its qualities is compassion to all living beings. I went out of my way to research companies that followed ecologically sustainable and fair trade practices. If I really liked their products, I would write great reviews and recommend them to others. I wrote to companies that had poor practices and told them why I was boycotting them. In my home and office, I placed stones and crystals that would hold those prayers and intentions. I did my best to follow through and work for—in a practical way—what I was asking for.

Some of you might refer to astrological events, others prefer to ask someone they trust for spiritual advice. When you create these traditions, keep them simple. The idea is that these will be rituals that you look forward to hosting and participating in. Be creative! Remember, these rituals represent *you* and the uniqueness of *your* space. If you find that a certain type of gathering becomes a chore or meaningless after a period of time, then it is perfectly okay to stop and develop a new one.

If you choose not to do any of this, nothing bad will happen to you. However, in time, spiritual energy may feel and become increasingly discordant with the turning of the years and with the people who dwell or work with you. What is of paramount importance here is to reinforce your values within your space that deepen the bonds of fellowship with family and friends and all of your helpers seen and unseen. Just as a strong body gives you the capacity to live a vibrant and dynamic life, the same is true for the energetic Heart of your place when you realign it with the Heart of the Earth.

Conclusion

BE PATIENT WITH YOURSELF, as mastering the Heart of the Earth method takes years of practice. I am sure that after completing the setting up of your space, which can seem arduous at first, you'll see that practicing this method is well worth your efforts. If you make maintaining your home a routine, you will see that it becomes essentially effortless to sustain it.

Keeping our connection to the Heart of our Earth Mother is not only our sacred responsibility, it is essential to our survival and to all species that share our precious world. One can live well while still actively working to conserve our ecology so that future generations may have clean air, sparkling water, and a green planet.

I know you will reap many advantages by living in harmony with nature. Greater peace, strong health, and steady prosperity are only some of the benefits that will lead you to living a more exuberant and satisfying life.

Appendix A

Reference List of Energetic Properties

Arrow: Spirit of the east

Compass Point Watched Over: East

Season: Spring

Time of Day: Dawn

Time of Life: Birth, infancy, young childhood

Time in Life Cycle or Project: New beginnings, finding focus, goals, setting energetics

Color: Red

Element: Fire

Animal/Material: Eagle

Gender: Male

Type of Energy: Point of stability

Qualities: Brings power to give light and life, new beginning, fresh start, seeing the greater picture, development of plans and goals, burning away of impurities or the past

Arrow: Spirit of the south
Compass Point Watched Over: South
Season: Summer
Time of Day: Midday
Time of Life: Youth, young adulthood
Time in Life Cycle or Project: Development, experimentation, expansion
Color: Yellow
Element: Air
Animal/Material: Coyote
Gender: Male
Type of Energy: Point of stability
Qualities: Boldness of youth, taking risks, finding one's soul tribe, expansion, planning for the future, trying new paths

Arrow: Spirit of the west
Compass Point Watched Over: West
Season: Autumn
Time of Day: Twilight
Time of Life: Middle age
Time in Life Cycle or Project: Growing deeper roots, reputation and practices
Color: Black/Navy blue
Element: Water
Animal/Material: Bear
Gender: Female
Type of Energy: Point of stability
Qualities: Well established, going further with what is important in life, introspection, connecting more profoundly with the Great Spirit, relationships, sacred beings, Sacred Self

Arrow: Spirit of the north
Compass Point Watched Over: North
Season: Winter
Time of Day: Midnight
Time of Life: Elder, old age, transition to spirit
Time in Life Cycle or Project: Letting go of an old life, closure, transitions
Color: White
Element: Earth
Animal/Material: Buffalo
Gender: Female
Type of Energy: Point of stability
Qualities: Sharing of wisdom, completions, connection of old generation with next generation, revisiting and updating of dreams and desires, leaving an old life behind

Arrow: Earth Mother
Compass Point Watched Over: Below
Season: Any
Time of Day: All
Time of Life: All
Time in Life Cycle or Project: Bringing plans into physical reality, feedback and refinement
Color: Green
Element: Physical
Animal/Material: All or any
Gender: Female
Type of Energy: Point of stability
Qualities: Divine feminine face of the Great Spirit, fertility in all of its forms, nurturing, empathy, large scale communication, community building, divine feminine wisdom

Arrow: Sky Father
Compass Point Watched Over: Above
Season: Any
Time of Day: All
Time of Life: All
Time in Life Cycle or Project: Planning and development, troubleshooting and solving
Color: Sky blue
Element: Spiritual
Animal/Material: All or any
Gender: Male
Type of Energy: Point of stability
Qualities: Divine masculine face of the Great Spirit, knowing when to speak and act and when to be silent and still, powerful protection, proper use of strength and power

Arrow: Great Spirit
Compass Point Watched Over: All
Season: All
Time of Day: All
Time of Life: All
Time in Life Cycle or Project: Oversees all, ensures that all stays on track
Color: All or any
Element: All or any
Animal/Material: All or any
Gender: All
Type of Energy: Point of stability
Qualities: In all things and beyond all things, unification, creation, Creator spirit, karmic understanding, brings harmony to discord, creates Heart

Arrow: None
Compass Point Watched Over: Northeast
Season: Winter
Time of Day: Midnight to dawn
Time of Life: Between lives, conception, gestation to birth
Time in Life Cycle or Project: Place of Becoming
Color: Pink
Element: Earth and fire (lava)
Animal/Material: Metals
Gender: Male
Type of Energy: Walking Wind, dynamic
Qualities: Infinite potential, brainstorming; no set focus, form or
    goals yet; seeker's journey, getting oriented in a new situation

Arrow: None
Compass Point Watched Over: Southeast
Season: Spring
Time of Day: Dawn to midday
Time of Life: Childhood to early youth
Time in Life Cycle or Project: Place of Self-Identity
Color: Orange
Element: Fire and air (lightning)
Animal/Material: Glass
Gender: Female
Type of Energy: Walking Wind, dynamic
Qualities: Discovery, experimentation, self-expression, seeing
    the world without limits or preconceived notions, innocence

Arrow: None
Compass Point Watched Over: Southwest
Season: Summer

Time of Day: Midday to twilight
Time of Life: Young adulthood to adulthood
Time in Life Cycle or Project: Place of Self-Empowerment
Color: Color of storms, yellowish black
Element: Air and water (hurricane)
Animal/Material: Textiles
Gender: Male
Type of Energy: Walking Wind, dynamic
Qualities: Gathering of power, resources, allies, information, building of reputation, family, career, manifestation, becoming established

Arrow: None
Compass Point Watched Over: Northwest
Season: Autumn
Time of Day: Twilight to midnight
Time of Life: Midlife to elder
Time in Life Cycle or Project: Place of Surrender
Color: Silver gray
Element: Water and earth (avalanche/mudslide)
Animal/Material: Wood
Gender: Female
Type of Energy: Walking Wind, dynamic
Qualities: Starting to let go of old roles and possessions, training next generation, reflecting on life and wisdom gained

Recommended Resources

HERE ARE THE BOOKS I mentioned earlier, but any books written by these authors are wonderful reference books!

Melody. *Love Is in the Earth: A Kaleidoscope of Crystals*. Wheat Ridge, CO: Earth-Love Publishing House, 1995.

Hall, Judy. *The Crystal Bible: A Definitive Guide to Crystals*. Cincinatti, OH: Walking Stick Press, 2003.

Berthold-Bond, Annie. *Clean & Green: The Complete Guide to Nontoxic and Environmentally Safe Housekeeping*. Woodstock, NY: Ceres Press, 1994.

I welcome you to contact me with any questions or thoughts. This book only covers the tip of the iceberg and in the future I will write more techniques beyond the basic ones covered here.

I encourage you to sign up for my newsletter. I do a weekly post called the "Flow of the River" and write about what to expect in the turning of the seasons and of the year. I am available for consultations in relation to helping you set up your home or work space using the Heart of the Earth method.

I also do traditional Native American readings to guide your life's journey. All services can be provided in person, by phone, by email, or virtually as I deem appropriate. I am willing to consider traveling if my expenses are covered in addition to my fee for services. On my website you can also purchase the audio support for the Waterfall meditation in chapter 3.

I am continuously offering classes on intuitive development, Native American shamanism, the Heart of the Earth method, soul work, and several other topics. Classes can be held in a group setting or one-on-one mentoring sessions. These too can be done in person, by phone, or virtually. Check in frequently as I am constantly developing new programs and in the future will have an apprenticeship program. You can contact me through my website at eagleskyfire.com and by social media.

I am very grateful for your support and for sharing time with me as you read this book. May your path be blessed with harmony, abundance, and joy. It is finished! *Dane-ho! Wanishi!*

Bibliography

Association of Nature and Forest Therapy Guides and Programs. "What is Forest Therapy?" Accessed July 7, 2020. https:// www.natureandforesttherapy.org/about/the-practice-of -forest-therapy.

Berthold-Bond, Annie. *Clean & Green: The Complete Guide to Nontoxic and Environmentally Safe Housekeeping.* Woodstock, NY: Ceres Press, 1994.

Driessnack, Martha. "Children and Nature-Deficit Disorder." *Journal for Specialists in Pediatric Nursing* 14, no. 1 (January 2009): 73–5. https://search.proquest.com/openview /a987ec02528b8b51140c9486b2ff8431/1?pq-origsite= gscholar&cbl=25318.

Evans, Karin. "Why Forest Bathing Is Good for Your Health." *Greater Good Magazine,* August 20, 2018. https://greatergood .berkeley.edu/article/item/why_forest_bathing_is_good_for _your_health.

Heerwagen, Judith. "Biophilia, Health, and Well-Being." In *Restorative Commons: Creating Health and Well-Being through*

Urban Landscapes, edited by Lindsay Campbell and Anne Wiesen, 38–57. New Town Square, PA: USDA Forest Service, 2009. https://www.nrs.fs.fed.us/pubs/gtr/gtr-nrs-p-39papers /04-heerwagen-p-39.pdf.

Kuo, Frances E., and Andrea Faber Taylor. "A Potential Natural Treatment for Attention-Deficit/Hyperactivity Disorder: Evidence From a National Study." *American Journal of Public Health* 94, no. 9 (September 1, 2004): 1580–1586. https://doi .org/10.2105/AJPH.94.9.1580.

Kuo, Frances E., and William C. Sullivan. "Environment and Crime In the Inner City: Does Vegetation Reduce Crime?" *Environment and Behavior* 33, no. 3 (May 1, 2001): 343–367. https://doi.org/10.1177/0013916501333002.

Kuo, Ming, William Sullivan, Rebekah Coley, and Liesette Brunson. "Fertile Ground for Community: Inner-City Neighborhood Common Spaces." *American Journal of Community Psychology* 26, no. 6 (December 1998): 823–51. https://doi .org/10.1023/A:1022294028903.

Livni, Ephrat. "The Japanese Practice of 'Forest Bathing' Is Scientifically Proven to Improve Your Health." Quartz. October 12, 2016. https://qz.com/804022/health-benefits -japanese-forest-bathing/.

Louv, Richard. *Last Child in the Woods: Saving Our Children from Nature-Deficit Disorder.* Chapel Hill, North Carolina: Algonquin Books, 2005.

Maller, Cecily J., Claire Henderson-Wilson, Mardie Townsend. "Rediscovering Nature in Everyday Settings: Or How to Create Healthy Environments and Healthy People." *EcoHealth* 6, no. 4 (December 2009): 553–56. https://doi.org/ 10.1007 /s10393-010-0282-5.

Minard, Anne. "Shampoo, Cosmetics May Form Cancer-Causing Substance in Water Supplies." *National Geographic*, May 1, 2010. https://www.nationalgeographic.com /news/2010/5/100429-shampoo-cancer-causing-substance/ #close.

Shanahan, Danielle F., Richard A. Fuller, Robert Bush, Brenda B. Lin, and Kevin J. Gaston. "The Health Benefits of Urban Nature: How Much Do We Need?" *BioScience* 65, no. 5 (April 2015): 476–85. https://doi.org/10.1093/biosci/biv032.

Tsunetsugu, Yuko, Bum-Jin Park, and Yoshifumi Miyazaki. "Trends in Research Related to 'Shinrin-yoku' (Taking In the Forest Atmosphere or Forest Bathing) in Japan." *Environmental Health and Preventive Medicine* 15, no. 27 (July 2009). https://doi.org/10.1007/s12199-009-0091-z.

Ulrich, Roger S. "View Through a Window May Influence Recovery from Surgery." *Science* 224 (April 27, 1984): 420–22. https://pdfs.semanticscholar.org/43df /b42bc2f7b212eb288d2e7be289d251f15bfd.pdf.